Towards a
Reconstruction
of
Macroeconomics

Towards a Reconstruction of Macroeconomics

Problems of Theory and Policy

~~

William Fellner

American Enterprise Institute
Yale University, Emeritus

American Enterprise Institute for Public Policy Research
Washington, D.C.

ISBN 0-8447-1318-X

Library of Congress Catalog Card No. 76-21162

Printed in the United States of America

To Laura,
whose generation will have
the benefit of hindsight on these problems
and should please be tolerant with us
who did not have it.

Table of Contents

Preface

Many of the problems discussed in these pages were briefly touched upon in a recent article of mine published in the *Journal of Economic Literature*.[1] But in the article these problems were merely touched upon, while in this volume quite a bit of elaboration will be found. The analysis is based on the empirical information I consider relevant.

Also, several problems will be discussed here that remained completely outside the scope of that article. The book includes, for example, an attempt to come to grips with the difference between "neo-Keynesian" and "monetarist" leanings in macrotheory, because I believe that in its present stage that controversy has many confusing aspects. Further, the reader will find in the volume my interpretation of the valid core of the hypothesis of the "induced bias" in innovation theory. The theoretical and empirical analysis of that problem is presented here in a framework in which the variable-proportions properties of the so-called neoclassical production functions are viewed as resulting from inventions and their industrial application (innovations) rather than as developing at a "given" level of technological and organizational knowledge. I need not go on surveying the problems discussed in the book, since the Table of Contents is fairly detailed.

While working on this book in Washington, I had the benefit of continuous professional contacts with economists in whom productive scholarship and academic interests have become

---

[1] "Lessons from the Failure of Demand-Management Policies: A Look at the Theoretical Foundations," *Journal of Economic Literature*, March 1976, pp. 34-53.

blended with expertise in the appraisal of available current information on the American economy. I must express my particular gratitude to Arthur M. Okun for the constructive and detailed suggestions I received from him when the first draft of the volume was finished. With at least one conclusion presented in the volume he is known to disagree (and he might disagree with more). Okun does not share my great skepticism about what I call the intermediate area between comprehensive wage and price regulations on the one hand and complete abstention from administrative wage and price controls on the other. Or, at least, he is much more hopeful than I am that ad hoc cost-price policies, bearing directly on money-wage and price trends, could be made effective and would not have the consequences discussed in my analysis. This disagreement relates to a matter about which we both have strong convictions. Yet we both seem to have the equally strong conviction that, regardless of how firmly our own views are held, they are not the only professional views that deserve to be expressed and articulated.

For valuable help in completing the research on which the analysis in this book is based, as well as for preparing the typescript, my thanks go to Waltraud Anderson.

Washington, D. C.
May 1976

I

The Main Theme
and the Nature of the Approach

1. Sketching the Content

This book has a thesis, and since it is a short book I hope that the thesis will become clear to the reader. An even briefer summary than will be found in the pages of the volume runs the risk of distorting rather than clarifying, but I will try such a further abridgement because this is necessary in order to get a methodological question out of our way at the outset. To do this requires saying a few words about the main theme of the analysis even at this stage.

Macroeconomic theory, which owes a huge debt to Keynes's work of 1936, has a deficiency from which it should be freed to be useful for more than an analysis of the policy requirements of a past period with very special characteristics—the 1930s. A theory of macroeconomic equilibrium can easily be developed into a theory of equilibrium growth paths, and as such can serve as a valuable frame of reference, but only if it clearly recognizes that in the neighborhood of such a growth path there cannot occur significant and sustained deviations of actual movements of the price level from expected movements. The employment policy results and other economic and social consequences of major unexpected movements of the price level are exceedingly damaging, even if it takes a short while for the damage to be clearly observable. Keynes and the Keynesians have paid little attention to what this implies for economic theory as well as for policy. Their monetarist critics, who have shown awareness of the problem, have not placed it in the center of the debate on the fundamentals of macroeconomics and have not worked it out or clarified it sufficiently. The fact that the world has recently suffered the consequences of significant inflationary disturbances, which in the United States have by now lasted for about ten years and have grown exceedingly difficult to cope with, has much to do with the influence of a macroeconomic theory that has not been adequately reconstructed.

If demand management policies will not succeed in *conditioning* market expectations to a reasonably predictable behavior of the price level—that is, if the public's expectations will not be formed according to credible price-level targets of the authorities—then we shall be heading for comprehensively controlled societies, administered with reliance on significantly enlarged police power. The issue has by now become a dramatic one, and it is wrong to talk around such a crucial issue by using evasive terminology on controls. Implied in the conditioning effort that is required for avoiding a transition into such a state is the need to recognize that the relation of the authorities to the public has an essential *game-of-strategy* aspect.

The authorities must act on assumptions about the public's responses, and members of the public must act on their assumptions about the responses of other members of the public and on assumptions about the reactions of the authorities to these. It is not enough to recognize that "rational expectations" are formed in view of the presumptive future behavior of the authorities rather than simply on the basis of the past behavior of the variables to which the expectations relate. A further essential fact is that the public attaches probability judgments to the way the behavior of the authorities may become influenced by the behavior of the public itself.[1] This is why credibility is of utmost

---

[1] The position developed in this book about expectations overlaps significantly with the views underlying the "rational expectations" hypothesis, but the analysis I shall present implies also that the problems we need to face contain a crucial element of games strategy. The games-strategy element derives from a justified suspicion on the part of the public that it depends on the public's behavior whether the authorities will persist in their mode of behavior. Further, it will be explained why I consider it inadvisable

importance—a fact that has gradually become clearer to at least some policy makers, but that has not been recognized as an essential element of a usable macroeconomic theory.

In their behavior in such a strategy situation, the authorities must be aware that no demand management policy can be successful in trying to validate an expectational system such as develops in markets without regard to the price level objectives of the policy makers. To try to validate an internally inconsistent and unstable expectational system is a hopeless effort. Nor will the effort to condition the markets to sustainable price-level expectations be successful if the determination of the authorities lacks sufficient credibility, because in that case the effort will lead to protracted "stagflation" that, in turn, is apt to lead the authorities to give up. Lack of credibility is self-justifying.

This position involves rejecting recent policy procedures based on the idea that we should take for granted money-wage and price-setting practices that developed in view of the public's past price experience during an inflationary period; and that we should aim for the money GNP that corresponds to an acceptable real GNP and to an acceptable employment level, given such pricing behavior by the public. Except for a short-term payoff to policy makers which is provided by the temporary fooling effect of unanticipated inflation, such an "accommodating" policy has proved self-defeating. It is self-defeating because it renders the expectational system that is so accommodated unstable upward, thereby destabilizing the economy and giving rise subsequently to the high costs of suppressing an accelerating inflationary process. The so-called Phillips trade-off between inflation and unemployment is a purely short-run phenomenon that must not be allowed to serve as a basis for demand management policy.

Footnote 1 (continued)
to follow Lucas and Rapping [29], Sargent [44], and Sargent and Wallace [45] in connecting the hypothesis of rational expectations with the hypothesis of the "natural rate of unemployment." In my view the hypothesis of the natural rate of unemployment cannot be carried over from the theory of perfect competition to "given imperfections" of actual markets (on some implied and inevitably arbitrary definition of a state in which these imperfections remain "given").

Demand management through monetary and fiscal policy can prove successful only if it succeeds in conditioning the public's price level expectations by creating an environment of appropriate restraint to which decision makers in the markets must adjust to avoid heavy losses. To imply that markets will continue for long to be guided by the past price behavior observed during a period of lax policies, and will do so regardless of how firmly convinced the public is that there has been a change in policy, means building on assumptions that are not borne out by historical experience; these are the assumptions that provide excuses for postponing again and again the changeover from lax to sustainable policies. It is, of course, inevitable that the transition from a period in which the expectational system was allowed to "run wild" to a period of conditioned price-level expectations should involve uncomfortable adjustments; but the more the adjustments are postponed, the costlier they become. The question to what extent the discomfort of the adjustment can be reduced by a policy of gradualism will be considered later.

Macro-equilibrium requires that the output decisions in the markets should be guided by price level expectations to which the decision makers have become conditioned by those in charge of demand management policies (monetary and fiscal policies) and it requires that the behavior of the price level to which expectations have become geared should be a sustainable behavior that can in fact be validated by the appropriate policies. To repeat: it is hopeless to try to validate by means of policy measures a fluid expectational system that develops independently in the markets and is not grounded outside itself. If the economy is to move in the neighborhood of an equilibrium path, the expectational system needs to be anchored in consistently pursued objectives of demand management policy.

2. Combining Methods of Approach

These opening remarks suggest that what we are trying to do here is to focus on a state of macroeconomic equilibrium—a state that can be fitted into a sequence of similar states in a growing economy. A theory relating to macroeconomic equilibrium needs to be distinguished from a theory relating to disturbed states of the economic system. I believe it is desirable to draw this distinction and to focus the analysis accordingly. But to say this means, of course, recognizing limitations on our knowledge about the economy.

The reader will rightly tell himself that the economy in which we live is always in a disturbed state, and that not much can be gained from putting a theory of macro-equilibria in better shape if no method is offered for comparing reality with the theory's frame of reference. The answer given here is that it is possible to create the required link in a number of ways that are not mutually exclusive but that this, at the present stage of knowledge, can be done more or less successfully only by methods that lack the formal properties characteristic of a general theory. We can place confidence of a limited sort in various models employed by short-term forecasters, the more successful among whom invariably use loosely organized information and personal judgment in addition to their models. At the same time we may be inclined to recall on occasion the prototypes of cyclical developments that were described in the "old-fashioned" business cycle theories of the pre-econometric era, and we may try to make up our minds on which of these basic types—or which combination of them—is likely to guide us best in the actual circumstances in which we are encountering the problem. In the post-Keynesian era, Hicks—building in part on Samuelson's work [41]—contributed to business cycle theory along these lines but, in contrast to most older contributions, with reliance on mathematical analysis: he derived a basic type of possible cyclical sequences in a growing economy, using the multiplier and the acceleration principle as the main ingredients of his model [22]. Further, we may place a moderate degree of confidence in various advance indicators that may suggest continued expansion or contraction or turning points and that may give clues also as to whether the tendencies they identify are forceful. It is possible to combine these methods, and it is necessary to use at least one of them.

The now prevalent method of appraising dynamic paths and future prospects combines a careful look at the results obtained from econometric models with a substantial amount of ad hoc "judgmental" adjustment. We shall see that, particularly for money GNP, the results so obtained have certainly not been "all bad," but it would be wrong to claim that such results are derived from a general theory. They are derived from a loose combination of types of analysis, even though elements of the mix (the models of the professional forecasters) would be highly formalized and complex dynamic theories, were the need for significant ad hoc adjustments not recognized by all whose appraisals have proved useful.

On the other hand, we want a more general theory of macro-equilibria for describing the frame of reference to which we relate the actual course of our economies and the outcome of policy measures. A sequence of such macro-equilibria represented by a normal growth path is an abstraction expressing an undisturbed basic tendency, given the market structures of an economy. In this sequence the aggregate supply of goods and services at levels at which this supply is forthcoming in a "sustainable" fashion is determined in accordance with the available resources and their real supply prices, and aggregate demand is kept equal to the supply so determined. The idea of a basic tendency with these characteristics abstracts from a large number of complications that stand in the way of useful generalization about the detailed course of economic processes.

The objection that basic tendencies do not exist "in reality" is unconvincing inasmuch as these tendencies are quite generally sensed by a population unless large deviations from them last a long time. It is reasonable to regard the manifestation of such underlying tendencies as part of our experience. And it would not be convincing to argue that we should simply plead ignorance about mechanisms that might keep an economy in the neighborhood of a path represented by macro-equilibria. We are, of course, unable to specify all the variables essential to these mechanisms, and even less can we make dependable numerical estimates of the set of relevant parameters. But experience with periods of significant instability on the one hand and with periods approximating stability on the other does carry strong suggestions about the bearing of major categories of variables on the differences between periods. Sustained deviations of the actual from the expected price level clearly belong among the disequilibrating factors: they have no place in analytical constructs describing equilibrium paths which are to serve as acceptable frames of reference.

Keynes was aware of the distinction between presumptive conditions of macro-equilibria and a complete dynamic theory. What he tried to formalize was a theory of macro-equilibrium conceived as a single stage in a sequence of similar stages that may be viewed as elements of a growth path. Keynes did have quite a bit to say about disequilibria—a fact rightly emphasized in Leijonhufvud's work [28] and, largely under his influence, also in more recent contributions. But it would be a mistake to overlook the fact that the technical apparatus introduced in the *General Theory* is directed at a state of macro-equilibrium and that the observations presented in that work on disturbed states of the economy supplement the technical analysis at a much less formalized level. Two references will be sufficient to support this interpretation here.

When in Chapter 18 Keynes gave a summary of the *General Theory*—and called it a "restatement" of the theory's main content presented earlier—he was clearly explaining how the basic functions of his system determine the properties of an equilibrium state. That state is, of course, a state of "equilibrium" only in the sense that the economy settles down in it given the characteristics of the markets: nevertheless, despite Patinkin's criticism of this terminological practice [35], I find it useful so to interpret the concept of macro-equilibrium in the present analysis. Also, what Keynes does in Chapter 10 with the Multiplier is to explain the distinction between (1) the validity of the formula $\dfrac{dY}{dI} = \dfrac{1}{1 - \dfrac{dC}{dY}}$ as the expression of a relationship between equilibrium states with different values of I and thus with different Y and (2) the possibility of deriving that formula as the limit of a geometric progression which unfolds itself in the course of the dynamic process described earlier by Kahn [24]. Keynes was obviously using the concept in the first of these two senses. Indeed, in the *General Theory* he derived the formula without bringing in the "dynamics" reflected in the geometric progression that had been formulated by Kahn several years earlier. The comments Keynes added thereafter were intended to avoid the confusion that could be caused by a lack of understanding how Kahn, on the one hand, had arrived at the formula and how Keynes, on the other hand, was deriving it in his book in 1936. The formal apparatus of the book is that of an equilibrium theory, given the specific market characteristics described in the analysis.

Yet to follow through on the distinction between a theory of macroeconomic equilibria and the supplementary observations on disturbed paths does raise two problems calling for explanation before we turn to our detailed discussion.

(1) In the first place, there exist obvious reasons why at present a relatively "rigorous" analysis of macro-equilibrium cannot guide us if our approach does not also include a more loosely knit analysis of disturbed paths. We must start conditioning the price level expectations to policy objectives in a significantly disturbed state of the economy. Here the fact that we do not possess a rigorous theory of such paths does, of course, create a difficulty. The policy makers can overcome this difficulty only by developing a strategy about whose success past experience justifies a good deal of confidence even if it does not justify unconditional faith. Our substantive conclusion from this will be that if the best available strategy will not be used or if (contrary to reasonable expectations) the markets will destroy themselves by not responding to that strategy, then we will be moving towards comprehensively and uncomfortably controlled political and economic units. The strategy that must be employed for us to have a good chance of avoiding this outcome is one that has been used in all past stabilization efforts after major inflations, and that was used successfully in the United States even in the relatively recent past. It is a credible demand-management strategy which in the neighborhood of a normal growth path generates no more aggregate demand than is required for the normal growth rate of the economy, given the price level behavior to which the markets have become conditioned. More-

over, it is a strategy that calls for moving consistently toward this objective if the initial point of departure happens to be located at a considerable distance from the normal path. A theory of macro-equilibrium must postulate consistent conditioning of the markets' price level expectations in this sense. *The outlook for success of the conditioning effort cannot be read from statistical samples drawn from periods of a demand management which was lax and was generally known to be lax.* Such periods belong in a different world. The point is that we need to move out of that world, and that we can succeed in moving out of it only if we can convince the public that we shall persist in our effort.

The fact that we must move out of a different world to arrive in the neighborhood of macro-equilibria provides one reason that the general theory of such equilibria can be applied only in conjunction with looser approaches relating to disturbed states of the system.

(2) Secondly, even if we are considering an economy already located near its normal growth path, we must ask ourselves the technical question what it means to formalize a piece of analysis for states of macro-equilibrium if the formal framework ceases to be applicable when the system moves out of that state, so that a rigorous theory needs to be supplemented with much looser analysis. The two ways of looking at the world must touch somewhere, and one needs to see how they touch.

Any set of relations describing a state of macro-equilibrium inevitably implies information of a limited sort about what happens when the equilibrium requirements are not met and the system is out of equilibrium. Yet all that is inevitably implied in a theory of macro-equilibria, jointly with the requirements for equilibrium proper, is a description of what may be regarded as the first stage of the development that takes place when an economy ceases to satisfy the equilibrium conditions. For example, it may be inferred from the summary of the formal framework in Chapter 18 of Keynes's *General Theory* that if income has been overestimated by consumers then consumption will turn out to be higher (savings lower) in relation to realized income than would be suggested by the consumption function. Moreover, it may be inferred that if at the same time investors

9

have overestimated the demand for their product, then—as a result of unwanted inventory accumulation—realized investment will be higher than the investment that had been planned. Such circumstances set the stage for disequilibrium with the characteristics of a cyclical setback.

These propositions were brought out quite explicitly by Swedish economists whose ideas were also being developed in the 1930s, mostly in the Wicksellian tradition and independently of Keynes—but they can be inferred from the Keynesian apparatus as well, since any set of behavioral functions from which equilibrium conditions are derived necessarily suggests specific conclusions about the first-stage effect (impact effect) when those conditions are not met. However, it does not follow from this that the behavioral functions in question are specified in a way that makes them suitable for tracing the course of the economy touched off by failure to satisfy the equilibrium conditions. What such a system suggests is merely that if the disturbance is random, equilibrium will be restored at the initial level of activity along *some* route, while if the disturbance has been caused by shifts of the behavioral functions then equilibrium will become established at a different level along *some* route. To specify the route itself would be an exceedingly ambitious task. It is at this point that the looser approaches take over, unless we have an unwarranted degree of confidence in the mechanical application of dynamic econometric models.

With the emphasis placed in our analysis on appropriately conditioned price-level expectations, the limitation of macro-equilibrium systems to impact effects of the disequilibrating forces can be illustrated in a general way by Figure 1. The system to be presented in Chapter V will deal with these problems more completely than could be expected of a simple sketch of this kind.

Here $\bar{p}_e$ is the price level to which market expectations have become conditioned. If the policy variables are set at the right level, the aggregate demand equals $\bar{p}_e\overline{Q}$ and the actual sales are $\bar{p}_e\overline{S}$. The difference between $\overline{Q}$ and $\overline{S}$ leaves room for intended inventory accumulation. Such a construct conveys the information that if demand turns out to be smaller or greater than $\bar{p}_e\overline{Q}$,

Figure 1

MACRO-EQUILIBRIUM AND THE IMPACT EFFECT
OF DISEQUILIBRATING FORCES

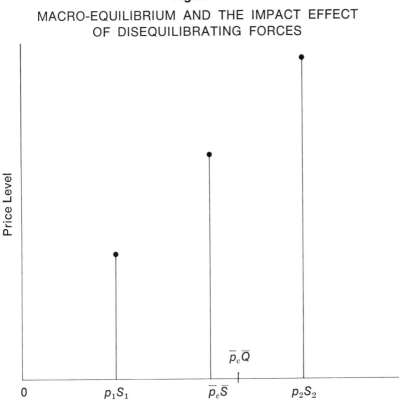

Market Value of Final Sales, Given the Output $\bar{Q}$

Legend: The output of the period is $\bar{Q}$; the expected aggregate demand is $\bar{p}_e\bar{Q}$. The expected real "final" sales (the output $\bar{Q}$ minus the expected inventory accumulation) is $\bar{S}$. The expected price level is $\bar{p}_e$. Note that $p_1 < \bar{p}_e < p_2$; also $S_1 < \bar{S} < S_2$; thus the left-hand point in the diagram expresses real sales that fall short of $\bar{S}$ at a price level located below $\bar{p}_e$, and the contrary is true of the right-hand point in both respects. The middle point describes sales when aggregate demand turns out to be $\bar{p}_e\bar{Q}$; the left-hand point when aggregate demand is smaller, the right-hand point when it is larger.

forces are generated that are apt to have *both* of two consequences: there will be an unintended accumulation or reduction of inventories (S will be smaller or greater than $\bar{S}$ depending on which of the two possible inequalities develop), *and* the actual price level will be lower or higher than $\bar{p}_e$. This is the impact effect of the disequilibrating forces. Yet a system of this sort is clearly not

11

rich enough to tell us what the path of the economy will be when expectations (including those relating to the future price level) will have changed. At the present stage of economic research, what happens in most cases is that government agencies and other economic experts try to make up their minds about the further course of events partly on the basis of econometric models that give unreliable results if not combined with ad hoc adjustments, and partly on the basis of such adjustments.

To aim for a predictable behavior of the price level and to be understood by the public to be pursuing that objective are necessary conditions for a successful demand-management policy. But they are not sufficient conditions. Success also requires that, given a demand management policy under which aggregate demand is adequate for an output compatible with the price level objective, demand not be used up for a shrinking output at rising prices. In a world in which neither the services of workers nor the commodities produced are supplied in perfect competition, and in which the reservation price of labor is strongly influenced by transfer payments available to those out of work, the policy effort could be blocked by these factors beyond a brief period of transition. However, if the policy effort remains consistent, the blocking behavior will, of course, become increasingly costly to the public and, in the event of a truly determined and credible policy, such behavior will hold only for a transition period of very limited duration. On the other hand, if the policy effort were not sufficiently consistent, the period during which the markets would not fall in line with the policy could be significantly extended, and this would make it increasingly difficult for the authorities to persist in their effort. In the end, blocking a policy effort that was aimed at a reasonably stable path of the economy would prove self-destructive: it would lead either to chaotic conditions or to comprehensively controlled political units in which there would be very little room for anyone to oppose the authorities. And it might lead first to the one and then to the other of these two results.

All these possibilities exist since, after all, historical trends are unpredictable. But it can be said with assurance that it is a foredoomed policy to generate inflationary trends and thereby keep the public in the belief that it will earn more than the available real income. Given our extensive network of transfer payments, and given our limited ability to interfere with market structures, the employment policy results obtainable under a policy of price level targets cannot be estimated quantitatively with much assurance, but it can be said firmly that over a reasonable length of time these results cannot be improved by inflationary policies.

Thus, as for the future, one possibility is that our policy makers will attempt to condition market expectations to price level objectives, and will succeed in their attempt—one hopes at or near the best activity levels compatible with that effort. The other possibility is a far-reaching political transformation, producing a significant concentration of additional power in the hands of central governments relying heavily on an enforcement apparatus and, on the way towards that concentration, quite possibly creating low productivity and disorder over an extended period of time. This volume is concerned mainly with the first of these two possibilities—that is, with the change from a demand management policy that has failed to one that can achieve reasonable objectives. There is as yet a very real chance of success along these lines, but this chance will fade if Western nations should continue to base their programs on slightly retouched forty-year-old theoretical foundations, constructed in the special historical circumstances of a different era. Those old foundations still contain much that is useful, but the professional work now needed is one of reconstruction rather than of retouching at the fringes.

3. Unconvincing Objections

I will end these introductory remarks with a brief presentation of the reasons I am unconvinced by two objections frequently encountered in discussions with my professional colleagues.

In the first place, it is often said there is little hope that wage and price behavior will adjust to demand policy objectives. This would suggest that the blocking of a reasonable policy effort would last long enough to make adoption of effective direct controls inevitable. But, as I said before, I am convinced that if this diagnosis should prove realistic, the reason would be the lack of consistency and credibility of the demand management policy declaring its determination to persist in creating no more aggregate demand than is called for by price level objectives and by the output movements compatible with these. It is essential to keep in mind that after all major inflationary interludes in economic history it is precisely the consistency and credibility of demand management efforts that made stabilization possible. It is equally essential to keep in mind that in the postwar United States until the second half of the 1960s the dismal view that the markets could and would keep sabotaging a price-level oriented demand-management policy would have been regarded as pure phantasy.

Try to visualize an environment in which it would again be fully believed that upward deviations from the known price-level targets of the authorities would impose a heavy penalty on all employers and a significant deterioration in the job outlook for workers. Each individual employer and worker or workers' representative would then have to tell himself: If in my small area I behave inconsistently with the general policy objective and many other individuals do the same in their areas, then business conditions will deteriorate greatly, and I will then regret my behavior; my main goal should then have been to avoid commitments that would make me share the exceedingly poor sales or employment outlook of the rest of the community. Alternatively, if while behaving inconsistently with the general policy objectives, I keep the possibility in mind that the others will not behave in the same way, then, too, I will regret my behavior because it will have led to a restriction of my sales volume *beyond* any degree that might (in some cases) reflect my increased market power. This latter consideration derives its justification from the fact that shifts in market power would come through even if the price level targets of the authorities were observed. To deny that the market environment can be shaped along these lines means to assert that the now relevant part of American economic history began in 1965. *Yet, what*

14

changed demonstrably about 1965 was the behavior of the policy makers, with no consistent or sufficiently pronounced signs of disillusionment on their part until very recently, and market behavior changed in response to policy changes. This will become clear as we go along.

Needless to say, one must be prepared to encounter hurdles on the way back from an accelerating inflation to a sustainable behavior of the price level, where "sustainable behavior" presumably means near-horizontality of the general price trend (though we shall see later that this specific interpretation of a viable price-level target does not follow cogently from basic economic analysis). Hurdles are encountered because at the start of the transition back to normalcy the determination of the authorities to persist may not yet be credible, but this is not the only reason. The other reason is that at the beginning of the transition process past commitments create for the sellers of goods and services a problem of trade-offs between (1) charging the costs developing from the past commitments and therefore losing sales volume and (2) not charging these costs in full for the sake of maintaining their sales volume at a more satisfactory level. Either choice is uncomfortable, and in some circumstances an economy on the way back to normalcy will indeed have to go through a period in which continued steep price increases are temporarily combined with a cyclical contraction of output. But if the policy effort is consistent, tomorrow's "past commitments" will cause the sellers smaller difficulties than today's and the transition period will not last long.

The more narrow-minded technicians—in contrast to the many who know how to blend their techniques with common sense—have a tendency to deny the validity of considerations such as these because they pretend that expectations depend on the lagged past behavior of variables without regard to the credibility of future policy action. But this view disregards the fact that the past behavior of all variables was also significantly influenced by expectations about the behavior of policy makers and thus by the credibility of the authorities' avowed objectives. For some time now the credibility of the authorities' anti-inflationary assertions has been extremely low in the United

States as in the rest of the world. In 1973 and 1974 inflationary expectations and the corresponding pricing practices were further strengthened by the widely held belief that by additional demand creation the authorities would and should "accommodate" inevitable burdens arising from partly natural and partly man-made supply limitations. Thereby the authorities would and should *ease* a "pass-through" of specific price changes with inflationary consequences for the general price level—as if such monetary accommodation could improve the position of those sectors on which the burden was imposed by a binding constraint. The obstinacy of inflationary money-wage and price-setting practices had a great deal to do with the known lack of obstinacy of the authorities in their pursuit of anti-inflationary objectives.

Another frequently heard objection to the position I take is that it overdramatizes the difference between a system that does and one that does not rely on direct wage and price controls. Between the comprehensive controls of the police state and abstention from the use of direct wage and price controls, it is argued, there is a large intermediate area. There does indeed exist a large intermediate area, but it is practically certain to prove an area of demoralization and low performance. It is possible to threaten with wage and price controls and not to adopt them, or to adopt them in form but not to enforce them; it is possible to enforce them haphazardly on rare occasions more or less at random; last but not least, it is possible to enforce them against those who are unpopular with the average voter or with the press, but not against others. But if demoralization of the society is to be avoided, one should surely be careful about when and how the penal system is used and against whom and how its use is threatened. The intermediate area between comprehensive wage and price controls and reliance on demand management policies without direct controls is highly objectionable, even if not objectionable in precisely the same sense as a well-organized and thoroughly policed system of political and economic control. It is remarkable how many euphemisms—ranging from "jawboning" to "social consensus"—have cropped up in recent years for hiding the true character of that large intermediate area. We have here the latest version of George Orwell's "Newspeak"

16

for describing spotty and haphazard interferences by which uncertainty can be raised to an exceedingly high level throughout the economy.

With respect to economic efficiency, the main difficulty with direct wage and price controls under democratic political institutions is that, to the extent that the controls are enforced, the wage and price structure is regulated with a view to the next elections and the decisions about the "appropriate" profits on successful but often very risky innovations are likewise politically inspired. In such circumstances market forces play a much smaller role in determining the outcome than is the case in a reasonably well functioning market economy. Occasionally proposed tax incentives or tax penalties for preventing inflationary money-wage increases are vulnerable to the same criticism, since such incentives or penalties must postulate a desirable wage and price *structure*, with substantial economic or legal penalties imposed on those who behave differently under the influence of market forces.

Unless market power is made or allowed to grow very large, its ability to distort the forces of competition is significantly smaller than that of governments that engage in the regulation of the wage and price structure. Democratic political institutions create no safeguards in this respect because deciding highly complex technical matters with vote-getting objectives in mind must lead to bad results. Only by undue stretching of any acceptable concept of equity could it be claimed that such politically inspired results represent a sacrifice of efficiency for the sake of equity—all the less so because, in a large country living under democratic institutions, spottiness of the enforcement effort can be taken for granted. In some small countries the difficulties may be reduced by the fact that, given reasonably free trade, the forces generated across the borders play a decisive role and these forces cannot be distorted by the domestic political process. Nor is the enforcement problem as difficult in small as in large countries. But the fate of the world will not be decided by the small countries, and this book was written in one that is large.

Basically, we have the choice between (1) conditioning market expectations to a behavior of the price level which, when it comes to be anticipated by the public, can be enforced by demand management policy, and (2) quite thoroughly changing the characteristics of our economic and political system. Macroeconomic theory will gradually have to be reconstructed in such a way as to take this into account. This volume represents a move in that direction, and I hope that it will not remain the only move.

I hope also that the analysis of these problems will recognize two facts reflecting the elements of strategy in the relations between the authorities and the population. One of these is that, while recessions resulting from the required demand-policy restraint in times of inflationary wage-price behavior will become rarer if the willingness of the authorities to resort to such restraint is generally anticipated, occasions will nevertheless recur when that willingness will have to be demonstrated at the cost of a cyclical setback. The other fact is that any manageable method of subsidizing the needy by guaranteed (or quasi-guaranteed) subsistence requires safeguards against misuse. Therefore, in the strategy situation that must be taken for granted, a government's ability to live up to "guaranteed" subsistence as a general rule requires determination not to live up to it in individual cases in which there is a sufficient presumption that the alleged need has developed because the individual was planning to rely on the guarantee. There is no way of formulating detailed prescriptions for a reasonable application of these principles, but this same negative statement can be made about most relevant problems of strategy—problems that have nevertheless often been faced successfully once their essential properties were recognized. In the main part of my analysis I shall return to what I consider the essential properties of the problems that give rise to these considerations of strategy. It will also be explained why in my appraisal these considerations strongly favor choosing approximate horizontality of the price trend as the target towards which policy makers should be moving consistently—a target that was in fact achieved during part of our postwar history, probably at the cost of more cyclical instability than would be inevitable in the future.

II
Fundamentals in an
Elementary Analytical Framework

1. The Reorientation of Macro-Theory during the 1930s

The macro-approach to the economic process is characterized by the use of broad aggregates, including output as a whole. Some degree of formalization of macro-relations is at least as old as simple quantity-theoretical constructs.

Among these constructs, that represented by the "Cambridge equation," $M = kpQ$, should mainly be kept in mind for our purposes.[1] If the symbols in the equation are interpreted as standing for the values of variables actually observed for a past period, the equation is a mere tautology. The stock of money (M) can always be expressed as some proportion (k) of the product of price (p) with the output (Q) produced during a given period—say, a year. Nothing essential is conveyed by this. But if k is interpreted as the *desired* ratio of money holdings to the value of the output produced (and acquired) during a given period, the equation expresses a useful supply-demand condition. The equation then postulates the equality of the supply of money (the M stock) with the demand for it, where the demand is expressed as the desired fraction k of the value of the output flow produced and acquired (pQ).

---

[1] The principal reference here is to Marshall, *Money, Credit and Commerce* [30]. It needs to be added that Marshall seems to have used this approach in Cambridge for several decades prior to the publication of that book in 1923.

When the supply-demand equation for money is written in this simplified form and is used as a single equation torn out of a broader context, it implies deliberate neglect of the fact that the demand for money per unit of output depends *inter alia* on the physical capital existing in the economy and on the terms on which other liquid assets are available to the public. In this form, the equation also implies that we are deliberately neglecting the fact that expenditures not representing "acquisition of output," and yet requiring the holding of a money stock, may fail to bear a fixed proportion to expenditures on "output." This holds regardless of whether the equation is used with Q expressing gross output (say, in the sense of the GNP) or is used with Q expressing net output (say, in the sense of the NNP). Money is used also for the purchase of goods and services that are not included in the current period's output in any sense and for the purchase of securities. To these problems we shall return later.

If, meanwhile, we continue with the simple money supply-demand equation $M = kpQ$, we are thereby also expressing $M/k = pQ$ as a condition of the equality of desired expenditures on current output (left-hand side) with the value of the output supplied (right-hand side). Considering that "velocity" concepts are reciprocals of k concepts, the equation could also be written as $MV = pQ$, but it is awkward to attribute to V the meaning of a "desired" velocity, while there is nothing peculiar about defining desired expenditures as the fraction k of the M stock. This much "macroeconomics" has a long history. So does the view that if, at a given level of p, the demand for current output expressed as M/k has become insufficient for matching Q of a size considered normal, then waiting for p to decline and for Q to rise correspondingly, instead of augmenting M/k, may involve a drawn out and uncomfortable adjustment process. Meanwhile, the demand for money per unit of expenditures—thus the k ratio—is apt to rise, as long as the risk of further price declines is considered substantial. Before the adjustment, the deflationary process may thus feed on itself for some time. Recognition of this leads to stressing the importance of demand management policies—monetary and fiscal policies—affecting M/k

20

through the influence of these policies on aggregate demand measured in "current dollars."

Keynes developed the analytical framework of the *General Theory* in the critical circumstances of the 1930s—circumstances that those who have not lived through that period may have a hard time visualizing. Expressed in terms of the simple quantity-theoretical framework here used as an expository device, the Keynesian system had two novel properties. One of these is that by formalizing relations among economic variables on the assumption of a given money-wage rate, it suggested the usefulness of an approach that excludes outright the possibility of achieving a desired upward adjustment of some period's subnormal Q by the deflationary method of allowing p to decline instead of raising M/k. The other is that the system made room for the analysis of conditions under which a needed increase in M/k can be brought about only by fiscal policy but cannot be achieved by the conventional central-bank technique of security acquisitions by the monetary authority (that is, by the purchase of government securities or by discounting bills or by making advances), because these conventional central-bank techniques would raise k in the same proportion as M. The second of these properties of the Keynesian system—the potential lack of effectiveness of conventional central-bank techniques—can be realistic only in very special circumstances and it usually requires little attention. The first of the two properties—the outright exclusion of deflationary adjustment processes from the formal system—does deserve to be emphasized.

According to the appraisal that will be suggested in the present volume, Keynes expressed an important insight when he suggested that the macro-theoretical apparatus can be simplified, and can be made more useful for many analytical purposes, by excluding from it the downward flexibility of the general price level. Generating unanticipated price deflation is clearly incompatible with keeping an economy in macro-equilibrium or in the neighborhood of a path described by a sequence of such equilibria, and such a policy is ill-suited to restoring equilibrium with minimum discomfort once a disturbance has occurred. However, the same negative statements apply also to the generating of

21

unanticipated inflation. The problem cannot simply be dispensed with by constructing a model which is foolproof against being used for the advocacy of deflationary adjustments, as Keynes's is.

2. The Imprint of a Past Era

The 1930s were not simply a painful episode in world history. In the interpretation of that period and of its sequels it is proper to place the events in Germany in the center of the story, but there is more to the story than its center. The ending of parliamentary rule in Germany and Hitler's coming to power early in 1933 resulted in very large part from the extraordinarily high German unemployment of that period, even if the expropriation of much of the middle class through the hyperinflation following World War I must also be taken into account in interpreting the German political upheavals. Whatever other circumstances may have played a role in the turn of events in Germany, and whatever other mistakes may have acquired importance in shaping the history of the subsequent decades, it remains true that for the 1930s any reasonable observer will be inclined to attribute more than the usual importance to conjectural history: without the Great Depression no Nazi takeover, without the Nazi takeover no World War II, without World War II no iron curtain across Europe and none of the corollaries of the latter in our lifetime.

Yet the developments originating in Germany are not the only developments deserving attention here. During the 1930s and subsequently, significant changes took place in the economic and social structure of all Western democracies, and while some of these changes would doubtless have occurred even apart from the depression and the war, it is impossible to interpret that period in Western institutional history convincingly without placing much of the emphasis on the dramatic course of events during the depression. Also, it would be difficult to interpret the present stage of development of economic theory without recognizing that a new era started in the 1930s.

No firm answer can be suggested to the question to what extent the shock that developed in the 1930s was "objectively" greater than that to which Western economies were exposed in earlier contractive phases of business cycles (including two protracted depressions during the nineteenth century) and to what extent the social fabric of the Western nations had become more sensitive to shocks of any given magnitude. Both these circumstances played a role. We have, of course, much better data for the depression of the 1930s than for most earlier ones. For the United States these show, from 1929 to 1933, a 31 percent decline of constant-dollar ("real") GNP, a 24 percent decline in aggregate real employee compensation [2] earned by employees whose number declined by 19 percent, a much sharper decline of professional and of farm income, and a drop of corporate profits from about 11 percent of the national income to zero.[3] Consumer prices had fallen in those four years by 24 percent, the GNP deflator by 22 percent, and wholesale prices by 31 percent. Avoiding an inflationary price trend for that decade was clearly not a problem to which much attention had to be paid. Whereas in 1929 unemployment was 4 percent of the U.S. labor force, in 1933 it was 25 percent. As a result of the overvaluation of sterling when it was stabilized in the mid-1920s, the British already had a serious unemployment problem before the depression. Even before the cyclical downturn, they had unemployment rates in excess of 10 percent, and during the depression those rates rose to more than 20 percent. In neither country did unemployment decline to anything like a normal level during the 1930s.

The views voiced by Keynes for several years before the publication of the *General Theory* foreshadowed those that were to be incorporated into that work. Nevertheless, it is the *General Theory* that opened a new period in Western economic thought, inasmuch as the influence of Keynes's ideas is attributable largely to the fact that he worked his ideas into the systematic framework presented in that book. The book was unmistakably a product of the Great Depression, but it was a book by one of

---

[2] This implies correcting the nominal compensation by the consumer price index.

[3] This is a positive figure of negligible magnitude without the inventory valuation adjustment and a small negative figure with it.

the great figures in the history of economic thought, deserving very serious consideration regardless of its birth date.

Yet Keynes, who died prematurely within a year after the ending of World War II, had no chance of putting the new framework in shape for an era with different characteristics. Adjusting that system was a task that could be undertaken in different ways by economists with different inclinations. The problem has not been that of eliminating the influence of the Great Depression on the analytical framework, but that of placing that influence in perspective.

The current efforts directed at this objective suffer mostly from one of two weaknesses. Some aim at using the Keynesian contribution as a point of departure for the advocacy of direct wage and price controls, which is clearly not in the spirit of that contribution (see, for example, [27], p. 379). Others aim at cutting Keynes down to size—a misguided effort, because his size was very large. The present volume is motivated by the conviction that none of the various postwar reinterpretations has come to grips with the crucial problem that gives rise to the need for reinterpretation.

3. The Meaning of Say's Law in a Simple Quantity-Theoretical Framework

Whereas the game of finding in one section of the *General Theory* a passage that is inconsistent with a passage in another section was for a while going on with a moderate payoff for the participants, it is safe to say that what Keynes presented as the main theme of his analysis was indeed intended to be just that. It is clear from the introductory sections of the *General Theory* that the principal function of the analytical system Keynes constructed was to describe the determination of aggregate output and of employment on assumptions implying that Say's Law is a misleading proposition that needs to be eliminated from a useful macroeconomic theory.

In the terms of the equation $M/k = pQ$, the intended meaning of the classical assertion known as Say's Law was that *on the assumption of flexible prices* insufficiency of aggregate demand cannot in the long run keep Q at a reduced level involving involuntary underutilization of resources. In those circumstances p would automatically decline to the extent needed for assuring that any initially insufficient M/k should become sufficient for absorbing the capacity output (the "capacity Q") at reduced prices. This is the intended meaning of Say's Law, even though some critics have expressed doubts about the correctness of the interpretation because of various awkward (but unessential) ambiguities in classical writings about that law. Keynes was unconcerned with the ambiguities and looked at what he quite rightly regarded as the intended meaning of the proposition. I shall argue, however, that he was not conscious of all the essential characteristics of the deflationary adjustment *process* by which Say's Law would be validated in the long run if prices were fully flexible. The classical economists had paid no attention whatever to the need to specify that process, and hence in the classical writings proper the "Law" remained merely an *assertion*. While neoclassical economists did make progress in this regard, it remained for the economists of the twentieth century to explain the process fully. When the *General Theory* was written, the nature of the process behind the classical assertion named for Say had not yet been fully cleared up, and Keynes's rejection of the classical assertion rested in part on hazy views about the process that could validate it.

An essential part of the position that Keynes developed and formalized was not much affected by this particular shortcoming. He argued that a pragmatically useful analytical framework must leave no room for the possibility of allowing a depressed Q to rise through a decline in p, but must focus instead on how a depressed Q can be increased by increasing M/k; and on this important issue he was right. Yet, since his objections to Say's Law rested in part on his failure to see clearly how the process behind the law would work on its own assumptions, he believed he had established a *sui generis* case against unanticipated deflation without having to concern himself with unanticipated inflation. His apparatus thus enabled him to disregard one-half of the problem in what was intended to be a general theory. But whereas disregarding that half of the problem did have a short-run justification in the special circumstances in which the book was written, it has no justification in a general macro-theoretical system. By now it is surely time to give this matter the attention it deserves.

Keynes was, of course, by no means alone in forcefully opposing attempts to rely on deflationary methods of raising the level of output and employment. At that time Haberler and Pigou were among those who strongly emphasized the dangers of deflationary processes and advocated expansionary policies, though full clarification of the reasons why Say's Law would indeed be validated in the long run with flexible prices is partly the contribution of these same authors [19, 40] [4] and later particularly of Patinkin, who developed a much more comprehensive analysis of that problem [35]. In fact, many economists took a determined anti-deflationary position during and after the 1930s without rejecting, as Keynes did, the validity of Say's Law on the implied price-flexibility assumptions. However, many others, including influential experts, advocated deflationary adjustment efforts during the 1930s, and Keynes was probably the most influential and persuasive figure on the constructive side of the policy controversy of the decade. On the question of deflationary adjustment, the distinctive feature of the *General Theory* was reliance on the technique used by Alexander the Great when he came to the Gordian knot: Keynes simply cut Say's Law out of his formal framework. He thereby eliminated from the framework the deflationary adjustment process as a means of moving an economy out of a state of underutilization. On the other hand, he did not eliminate inflationary processes, to which he attributed an "equilibrating" property.

4. Basic Elements of the Keynesian System and the Cambridge Equation

In his formalized system Keynes got rid of Say's Law by postulating constancy of the money-wage rate and thus downward

---

[4] For Pigou's convictions about the need for expansionary policies in the 1930s, see Hutchison [23].

inflexibility of the price level. The formal apparatus being one of an equilibrium theory rather than one of dynamics, the exclusion of Say's Law shows formally in the fact that a Keynesian equilibrium state with higher employment does not have a lower money-wage rate and a lower price level than a Keynesian equilibrium state with lower employment; the equilibrium state with higher employment has the same money-wage rate, higher prices, and thus a lower real-wage rate. For our present purposes, it is necessary to go briefly over some details of the Keynesian apparatus, fitting the account into the main thread of our analysis.

In the Keynesian formal construct, for each potential level of income the interest rate is determined by the institutionally set supply of money and by the demand for it. This demand is smaller at low than at high interest rates because as the interest rate rises asset holders substitute securities for money in their portfolio. Given the interest rate, investment depends on the expected profitability of additions of various sizes to the capital stock, with allowances for risk (the marginal efficiency of investment). Finally, consumption is a function of income, where the latter equals output. The properties of these functions are specified in such a way that there exists a unique equilibrium output or income. This level of income satisfies the condition that the consumption forthcoming, plus the investment determined by the interest rate and the marginal efficiency of investment, should equal the income in question. This equilibrium income can therefore also be derived by multiplying the so-determined investment by a "multiplier" whose value depends exclusively on the amount of consumption forthcoming at alternative income levels—that is, on the consumption function.

Inasmuch as in Keynes's formal analytical system the money-wage rate ("wage unit") is the unit of measurement for all these magnitudes, the formalized theory is intended to apply only to ranges of output for which the money-wage rate can be assumed as given. *Contrary to what is often said and taught, this does not imply that in the ranges of output to which the theory is intended to apply the price level remains constant.* The p term of the "Cambridge equation" is rigid downward but not upward. Keynes was not only quite explicit but even emphatic in maintaining that real-wage rates can be reduced, and that the unemployment he defined as "involuntary" can thus be eliminated, by expansionary demand-management policies that raise the price level.[5] At higher real-wage rates the system would settle down at lower levels of output—that is, in "underemployment equilibrium." Keynes's state of macro-equilibrium is obviously meant to be a stage along a time path, though the consistency requirements for time paths were formulated by economists using and expanding the Keynesian framework rather than by Keynes himself.

Whereas Keynes did not employ the quantity-theory framework for expressing these ideas, it is useful to indicate the meaning of his ideas in terms of the equation $M = kpQ$ or $M/k = pQ$. The p term is inflexible downward. The k term is inversely related to the interest rate, and it grows significantly at very low rates of interest where very little loss of income is involved in holding money instead of securities. To keep Q at a level corresponding to full employment when it tends to fall below that level, M/k must be increased and this will raise p and thus reduce real wage rates. This is clearly the gist of Keynes's analytical result.

Whether in the Keynesian system it is possible to increase M/k by the conventional central-bank operations involving the acquisition of securities from private holders depends on whether the sellers of these securities, having acquired more money, make more expenditures. The usual central-bank techniques will prove ineffective if those from whom the monetary authority acquires securities for money hold the entire addition to their money stock idle in their portfolios, simply substituting this money for securities without raising their expenditures. This latter possibility—reflecting the "liquidity trap" or "absolute liquidity preference"—crops up in various parts of the Keynesian analysis. He represented the liquidity trap as devel-

---

[5] In other words, in the Keynesian system those "involuntarily unemployed" must accept a cut in their real wages resulting from such price increases, though they need not accept a cut in their money wages. We shall elaborate on the implications of this view in the subsequent discussion.

oping only at interest rates so low that the sellers of securities to the central bank would not need to be offered higher security prices to elicit security sales: as a result, the interest rate would not decline any further when the central bank expanded the money supply by its security acquisitions, and there would be no incentives provided for additional investment.

In the event of such a liquidity trap, M/k could not be increased by the conventional central-bank operations because in those circumstances such operations increase k in the same proportion as they increase M. However, even in the liquidity trap M/k could be increased by government expenditures—that is, by borrowing money from those willing to buy government securities and spending the proceeds in a fashion that created additional incomes. This is the case because the buyers of the government securities would substitute these securities for their money holdings, thereby diminishing the value of k, and those who derived additional income from the government expenditures would not increase their k ratio in relation to their income correspondingly.

In an economy not finding itself in the liquidity trap—that is, in an economy in which the interest rate has not hit a floor level—conventional expansionary central-bank operations will increase M/k, though these operations will increase k to some extent along with increasing M. The k ratio will be increased to some extent because of the lowering of the interest rate. Of such an economy it is also true that borrowing from the public for income-creating government expenditures will raise M/k, even at unchanging M, but outside the bounds of the liquidity trap this is not the only way of raising M/k; it is rather an alternative to raising M by the conventional money-creating operations of the central bank. The fiscal operations, which outside the bounds of the liquidity trap merely represent such an alternative, raise the interest rate (which in this case is not at a floor level). By raising the interest rate, these operations crowd out some amount of private investment, but they crowd out less than the amount equivalent to the government expenditure because the rise of the interest rate reduces k and thus raises M/k for any given M.

The main part of the story is that, with p inflexible downward, full employment (or the capacity level of output) can be achieved only by policy methods keeping M/k at the appropriate level. Emphasis is placed on the need to watch the effect of money-creating operations on k through the interest rates. The possibility of achieving the full employment level of Q by raising M/k is represented as resulting from the real-wage reducing effect of an increase in p—that is, of the price increase associated with the increase in M/k.

As was noted earlier, all reasonable interpretations of Say's Law are based on the idea that in the long run any arbitrarily fixed M will assure the Q involving full employment, by the automatic decline in p that takes place when the system falls below full employment. This mechanism is here put out of commission by the postulated downward inflexibility of the money-wage rate and hence of p. Macro-equilibrium can establish itself at or below full employment, depending on demand management policies, including fiscal as well as central bank operations impinging on M/k.

The behavior of the system outside macro-equilibrium is not formalized. Keynes's general discussion of dynamic processes suggests that if, for example, the economy is moved out of a high-level macro-equilibrium by a downward shift of the output-determining functions, or by a *ceteris paribus* lowering of M, then the system will tend toward macro-equilibrium involving a lower Q; but during the transition the public will not behave in accordance with the basic Keynesian functions that determine its behavior in equilibrium. These functions will, however, disclose the "first-stage" consequence of the disequilibrium—that is, the state developing before the public starts reacting to the disappointments suffered as a result of an excess of supply over demand. The basic functions will also disclose the characteristics of the new equilibrium toward which the system tends, but not the details of the process taking place while the public corrects the position into which it arrived temporarily as a result of the unexpected discrepancy between supply and demand. Ohlin, Lindahl, Lundberg, Myrdal, and others of the Swedish school [6]

---

[6] For a detailed discussion and specific references, see Haberler [19], p. 180.

explained the first-stage effect (impact effect) of an economy's being thrown off its equilibrium path more explicitly than did Keynes, and some of their contributions contain schematic (merely illustrative) descriptions of possible sequences of events in disequilibrium. As was noted in Chapter I, Hicks later demonstrated rigorously that by combining the Keynesian Multiplier with the acceleration principle a cyclical course can be described for a growing economy.

The initial Keynesian framework has been further developed by "neo-Keynesian" economists of the subsequent decades. Other economists—those regarded as monetarists—can either be said to have modified the Keynesian framework to a larger extent than the neo-Keynesians or to have modified the traditional quantity-theory framework in a way that takes account of the Keynesian and neo-Keynesian contributions. To these developments we shall return.

Later—in Chapter V—we shall also give an illustration of the way in which the position taken in the present volume can be formalized in the light of recent work. In terms of the initial Keynesian formulations the position to be taken here stresses that Keynes's hypothesis of the real-wage equilibrating effect of a rising price level is unsupported by the facts. The position to be developed here also stresses that the description of an equilibrium system must include the condition that the expected price level, $\bar{p}_c$, establishes itself in fact as a result of a demand management policy (monetary and fiscal policy) that has first successfully conditioned the markets to the expectation of $\bar{p}_c$. An output and employment level that is not forthcoming with this behavior of the price level is not an equilibrium level toward which the economy will tend, but a disequilibrium level which it is possible to achieve temporarily but which the authorities should try to avoid because of its aftermath. In the terms of the simple Cambridge equation we have been using so far for illustration, this amounts to writing the equilibrium condition as $M/k = \bar{p}_e Q$, where $\bar{p}_e$ was defined above and Q is the output forthcoming given the foreseen $\bar{p}_c$.

In such a system there is no room for any equilibrating effect of unforeseen price changes. While the system does not perform the ambitious task of covering events along disturbed (cyclical) paths with a claim to generality, no system stressing our price level condition for macro-equilibria could convincingly suggest dealing with underutilization by generating unexpected deflationary price movements, or by allowing these to develop.

5. Income-Expenditure or Stock-to-Expenditure Approach?

It has become conventional, but on the whole more confusing than revealing, to describe the Keynesian system as representing an income-expenditure approach—both income and expenditure being "flow" concepts—and to draw a contrast between such an approach and approaches suggesting that expenditures are determined by desired ratios of *stocks of wealth* to the spending flow. This latter stock-to-flow approach is illustrated in its simplest form by $M = kpQ$, where we should keep it in mind that the variables on which the public's desired value of the stock-to-flow ratio defined as k depends include the existing stock of physical capital and the terms of availability of liquid assets other than money (hence also the interest rate).

To draw a contrast in this form provides no useful guidance for appraising these approaches. In the first place, in the Keynesian framework investment is an expenditure determined not by income but by the profitability of enlarging the exist- ing stock of physical capital, given the interest rate and with allowances made for risk. Consumption expenditure *is* viewed as undertaken out of income, but to say this is no different from saying that a person receiving the kind of regular stream re- garded as "income"—and thus either possessing personal income- earning capacity (which is in the nature of a "stock") or pos- sessing a stock of assets in the conventional sense—will establish some desired relation between the stocks he possesses and his consumption expenditures.

At a sufficiently rarefied level of abstraction we could "iden- tify" the stock-of-wealth equivalent of all income, including human capital (personal earning power) in the definition of wealth, and we could then pay no attention to income separately.

Account would have to be taken of the fact that the wealth equivalent of a current income depends on interest rates and also on how long the income stream is likely to be earned (Friedman's distinction between "permanent" and "transitory" income).[7] However, given the nature of the available data, observed wealth and income magnitudes are not useful proxies for one another, so that when we are concerned with the determinants of demand we should include both wealth and income among the explanatory variables. The stock of wealth is more fundamental, since if it could be measured accurately and in a sufficiently comprehensive way it would take into account the duration of the income flows of which it represents the mirror image. Regarding both income and wealth as determinants of aggregate demand has the characteristics of a "makeshift," but as such it is indispensable.

In Chapter V we shall in fact use a continued income flow as one explanatory variable of expenditures on output, and shall use assets (not including human capital) as another explanatory variable. But this will not place our model in an income-expenditure category rather than a wealth-expenditure category or the other way around. Nor does the problem of primary interest to us—the problem of the price level requirements of macro-equilibrium—shape up differently according to whether the point of departure for a more fully developed framework is the initial Keynesian or one that is quantity-theoretical. However, on the very simple level of formalization at which we have been working so far it is easier to direct attention to price level behavior with reference to the p term of the quantity-theoretical constructs than with reference to the Keynesian theory as originally presented.

6. Interdependence with the Rest of the World

Much of the debate about macroeconomic approaches that was touched off by the Keynesian contribution in the 1930s treats individual countries as if their demand management policies

---

[7] See particularly [11], and also Modigliani and Brumberg [31].

could afford to disregard the policies adopted in other countries. More recently, the awareness of international interdependences has been spreading, all the more because the volume of international trade has been rising more steeply than the national income of most countries. We shall not focus on these interdependences, but since what has been said so far has an isolationist flavor, it is time to take at least a brief look at the nature of the amendments and qualifications required in view of the relations of countries with the rest of the world.

In a world with fixed exchange rates and integrated markets, countries could not in general aim at individual price-level targets. This proposition is subject to the qualification that it does not apply to a country whose currency is used by the other countries as an international reserve, and is so used to such an extent that for this country, when it has run out of its own reserve assets, any further outflow of reserves merely means a transfer of domestic currency from domestic to foreign owners and an inflow merely means a transfer of domestic currency from foreign to domestic owners. The United States found itself in this special situation under the Bretton Woods system (which, however, collapsed in the early 1970s just because of the large accumulation by foreign owners of significantly overvalued dollars with a corresponding weakening of the American competitive position in the world market). A country not in this special situation cannot normally prevent sustained reserve inflows from having expansionary effects, and it certainly cannot prevent sustained reserve outflows from having contractionary effects. Thus an increase or decrease in the money supply brought about by the central bank of a country would come to be distributed over the fixed-rate community.

Autonomous price-level objectives can, however, be successfully pursued under flexible exchange rates, with the appropriate domestic monetary policy. The domestic policy required for divorcing the trend in the domestic price level from a changed trend in foreign prices *may* involve a reduction of the domestic level of activity—but only if such a reduction is inevitable in any event because in the changed circumstances the domestic economy will not observe its balance-of-payments constraint at the initial level of activity.

As for the bearing of the exchange-rate regime on the effectiveness of "managing" aggregate demand, opening up a closed economy under fixed rates will reduce the domestic expansionary demand effect of a growing money supply for the same reasons that make the price effects of money growth spread across the borders by means of reserve movements. The analogous statement holds for the demand effects of monetary restraint. Turning from monetary policy to fiscal expansion with no money growth: we may say that under fixed rates the price effects of such a policy will also be spreading internationally, but the initiating country will for some time capture more of the total expansionary effect than will the initiating country relying on monetary expansion. The reason is that there will be a period during which the upward pressure on domestic interest rates will be pulling in foreign capital and reserve assets. The analogous statement holds for fiscal restraint.

The remarks in the preceding paragraph apply to a system of fixed exchange rates. To open up a closed economy under flexible rates does not reduce the effectiveness of monetary policy because (to illustrate with expansionary operations) the initiating country will experience no reserve outflow but will instead experience a decline in its currency rates abroad. Indeed, the decline of the currency rate may for some time be magnified by capital exports as a result of a downward pressure on domestic interest rates—a reinforcing expansionary effect of monetary policy. On the other hand, in the event of fiscal expansion with no money growth under flexible rates, the upward pressure on domestic interest rates is apt to call forth capital imports that will for some time work counter to the forces reducing the domestic currency rates. Consequently, the upward pressure on interest rates is apt to weaken rather than reinforce the expansionary effect. Thus, when we move from fixed to flexible rates the case for monetary policy is strengthened in comparison with the case for fiscal policy, at least when the latter concentrates on the expenditures side of the budget.[8]

---

[8] On these problems see particularly Sohmen [45] and Mundell [32].

What interests us most in the present context is that under flexible rates a country can adopt independent price-level objectives—something it cannot do under fixed rates. We shall assume in the main part of our analysis that the political unit we are considering can pursue its price level objectives successfully— either because it has flexible exchange rates or because its demand management policies are coordinated with other countries over a major area within which exchange rates are fixed. For the special purpose of the formalization in which we shall engage in Chapter V, the assumptions concerning exchange rates will be made more specific.

III

Employment Theory and the Price Level

1. Generalization of the Argument against Reliance on Say's Law

Need for a consistent effort to condition the markets to a predictable behavior of the general price level—to a behavior that can be validated by demand management policy—clearly does not suggest reliance on adjustment processes that would generate large unexpected movements of the general price level. Yet, reliance on the self-equilibrating process implied by Say's Law would lead to price movements of this sort. The analysis in this volume emphasizes the fact that the resulting negative appraisal of policies based on Say's Law and the resulting anti-deflationary propositions merely make up the message written on one of the two sides of a coin, while the other side contains an anti-inflationary message. The true meaning of these messages is that a policy determined to condition price level expectations will greatly complicate its task if it permits or promotes interludes in which the behavior of the price level is unguided by demand management and is essentially "running wild." The conventional presentation of the problem does not bring out the general case against major unexpected movements of the price level, and Keynes in particular argued that there is more to it than is here suggested when it comes to the rejection of deflationary adjustment and less to it on the inflationary side. We shall see why this is unconvincing.

2. Valid Description of the Process behind Say's Law

The proposition that has become known as Say's Law, and that in the classical writings was a mere assertion, was considered valid by a long line of economists belonging to the classical school, beginning with Adam Smith. It was named for Jean-Baptiste Say because of his very vocal advocacy of the proposition, in particular against Malthus who did not believe in it.[1] In modern discussions of the history of the problem, much has been made of the fact that the various classical assertions of the "Law" differed from each other in content. Some economists are inclined to the view that we should abstain from referring to Say's Law because such references are apt to become confusing, but I consider that degree of skepticism unjustified. Keynes, among others, knew well what proposition the classical economists meant to assert. It is an essential proposition.

The intended meaning clearly was that an economy could not suffer from a deficiency of total effective demand measured

---

[1] The numbered bibliographical references attached to this volume do not include any of the long list of writings of the classical school that support the statement in the text.

The proposition attributed to Adam Smith in the subsequent pages is found in Book II, Chapter III, of the *Wealth of Nations* (1776). In the discussion of the history of this problem the reference to Smith is almost always omitted from the relevant sources—wrongly so. For Say's strong stand on the position associated with his name, see, for example, Book I, Chapter XV, of his *Traité d'Economie Politique* (1803), and perhaps particularly his later *Letters to Malthus* (1821). The argument developed in Book III, Chapters XII and XIV, of John Stuart Mill's *Principles of Political Economy* (first ed. 1848) suggests that (at least by 1848) Mill was trying to draw a sharp distinction between the short- and long-run validity of Say's Law and that he was asserting its long-run validity. To my mind Patinkin is right in attributing a similar long-run interpretation of Say's Law to Ricardo, who asserted the validity of the "Law" in his *Principles of Political Economy* (first ed. 1817), as well as in his correspondence with Malthus.

against the requirements of capacity production. This interpretation of the "Law" follows from the fact that in the writings of all the major economists of the classical school who asserted the proposition, it was used to support the claim that there is no such thing as a *general glut*, or general overproduction. Discrepancies between the demand mix and the output mix could, it was argued, lead to *partial* overproduction of specific goods relative to others and could thereby give the impression of a general glut. But this would be a false impression.

It is quite true that the various classical statements are in part hazy and that some of the statements express propositions that any contemporary economist would distinguish from the intended one. This, however, is true of many eighteenth century and early nineteenth century formulations which in their tightened-up versions would now be called theorems. The classical economists were best at expressing the intended meaning of Say's Law when asserting that supply inevitably creates the equivalent demand in the aggregate. Yet, instead of formulating it always in this way, they sometimes maintained that in reality goods exchange for goods and only apparently for money; or that not to spend the money collected for the commodities sold would be an irrational mode of behavior, and that such behavior does not acquire importance; or that receipts saved are spent as regularly as those which are not saved—the last of these being Adam Smith's way of putting it. These statements do not express the intended meaning nearly as well as the statement that supply creates the equivalent demand in the aggregate. But the context in which any of these assertions was made is always essentially the same: there can be no insufficiency of aggregate demand for enabling producers to raise output to the capacity level.

Keynes was rightly not bothered by the fact that many older economists sometimes did and at other times did not clearly formulate what they intended to assert. He interpreted them to mean what they truly meant. He was, of course, conscious of the failure of the classical school to specify the *process* which would lead to Say's results, yet he was aware also of subsequent discussions of the process during the neoclassical period, and in his critique of the "Law" he lumped together the classical and neoclassical economists, calling them all "classical" for this particular purpose. Thus, his critique of Say's Law was directed not merely at an assertion but at a process behind the assertion, as he interpreted that process. But because the analysis of the process involved was not particularly satisfactory until a somewhat later time,[2] Keynes found fault with it to which it is not in fact subject when it is properly described. Because of this, he argued that his own position on the "liquidity trap" would invalidate the description of the process behind Say's Law. He believed he had developed an anti-deflationary argument that had no anti-inflationary counterpart.

As we noted in Chapter II, if the interest rate declines to a very low level, the economy can be caught in a "liquidity trap"— the trap being defined by the inability of the monetary authority to induce additional spending by security acquisitions of the central bank. Such security purchases would merely result in the acquisition of idle (unspent) money by the public—merely in a rise in the k ratio—because the interest rate could not decline further, and no incentive would be created for increased investment. Keynes believed that this difficulty *could* develop at a future date, perhaps even in the not very distant future, as a result of diminishing physical returns to investment. But this conjecture of forty years ago shows no signs of being justified by what has happened since. On the other hand, when discussing the limitations of Say's Law, he attributed significance to the same difficulty *as of the time when he was writing,* that is, during the depression of the 1930s. He did recognize that if expansionary policies were not adopted and the general price level were allowed to decline, more liquidity in real terms would then indeed be created, because the real value of the existing stock of liquid assets would grow. This creation of liquidity, he observed, would lower the interest rate. But once the rate were lowered to a floor level, the economy would be caught in the liquidity trap, and the automatic adjustment process behind Say's Law would

---

[2] See the references on p. 26, and the detailed discussion of antecedents in [35].

cease to bring forth new spending. The additional expenditures brought about by the rise of the real value of liquid assets could, as a result, be far from sufficient to create the effective demand needed for raising output to the capacity level, or even for raising it much from the depressed level of the 1930s. The automatic deflationary process would be subject to the same limitations as the conventional expansionary central-bank policies, these being the limitations calling for the expansionary fiscal policies discussed in Chapter II.

Keynes was, of course, aware that a different kind of argument was needed for explaining why a liquidity trap might develop here not as a result of significantly reduced profitability of investment along a growth path but in a depression leading to a deflationary process. He argued that in such a situation the expectation that the interest rate would rise from its low depression level might lead the public to hold money rather than buy securities (and thus lend to investors)—given current security prices that are expected to decline. On the other hand, a belief that the interest rate would remain at a very low level would, as an element in a generally pessimistic expectational system, also impede economic recovery (see [27], Chapters 15 and 19).

Yet, quite apart from the question whether a decline of the interest rate to some floor level would in itself bring about the requisite additional expenditure by providing investors with cheap funds, the process behind Say's Law has another aspect to which Keynes paid no attention. An increase in the real value of liquid assets resulting from declining prices would raise the private wealth of the public—its command over goods—and if the process moved far enough, increasing amounts of *real* balances would be spent rather than simply accumulated as further reserves against future spending needs. In other words, "real balances" belong among the variables entering into the utility functions of the public. If the automatic adjustment process were to lead to an increasingly large addition to this specific utility-yielding item, the public would see to it that the entire increment to its possessions would not remain in this form, and other utility-yielding items would be acquired. Given the implied downward flexibility of prices under conditions of underutilization, this result would be achieved at the end of the process, even if the adjustment were delayed by a temporary rise in the k ratio while the likelihood of further price cuts was still considered high. It must be recognized that to the extent the liquid asset holdings of the public are offset by liabilities of the public itself, the real-balance effect so described does not hold. But the monetary base is not a liability of the public, nor does the government debt play the role of private indebtedness in the decision-making process of all spending units (even if in some sense the public does owe it as well as own it). While the problem was properly clarified only by contributions in recent decades—by Haberler, Pigou, and particularly by Patinkin—the clarification process had a good many neoclassical forerunners, Walras prominent among them [51].

The *dynamics* of the self-equilibrating process would be more involved than our brief account suggests. For example, while (as stated above) a deflationary process *increases* the real value of the available supply of liquid assets to the point where the requisite expenditures on goods are induced, it does so when the expectation that the price decline has come to an end *reduces* the demand for liquidity, and during the following expansion that demand is apt to become further reduced. The approach to equilibrium may therefore involve detours through phases of overshooting, caused by the cyclical behavior of the k ratio.

If we take account of these essential aspects of the real-balance effect, the process behind Say's Law becomes convincingly specified, so that further spending does not cease to be induced even if the interest rate falls to a floor level during the adjustment process. The hardships of the unanticipated deflationary process so described could, of course, be exceedingly severe—so severe that the political system might not survive the contraction needed to break the existing money-wage and price rigidities and thereby bring about the downward flexibility of money-wage rates and prices implied in the process behind Say's Law. But to say this is to raise a general objection against allowing major unexpected movements of the general price level to develop, regardless whether the movements are deflationary or inflationary. The objection is based on the fact that such price movements are apt to feed on themselves over an extended period, making it much more difficult to subject price level expectations to the necessary conditioning effort. In other words, this argument, in contrast to the false liquidity-trap objection against the process behind Say's Law, is not limited to the deflationary side of a general problem.

Even when the deflationary adjustment process is adequately described, there exists an apparent lack of symmetry between the deflationary and the inflationary side. Deflation could progress quite far with a constant supply of money, while it is much more difficult to imagine conditions under which inflation could so progress. But for our present purpose this asymmetry is irrelevant because the argument for relying on inflationary processes does *not* imply that the money supply would be kept constant. On the contrary, it implies that expansionary policies should deliberately induce price increases alleged to perform an "equilibrating" function. But a careful look at the argument leads us to conclude that the function such a policy performs is that of raising the level of activity merely as a result of the fact that the inflation so induced has an unexpected component; and that stabilization follows after a significant increase of effective demand brought about by expansionary demand-management policy when instability has already expressed itself in the acceleration of the inflationary process.

The dynamics of the stabilization process after accelerating inflation are complicated by factors partly analogous to those explained in connection with the "Sayian" deflationary adjustment (changes in the k ratio), but there are further difficulties here also for the reason that demand management policy (which in the inflationary case had not been simply "waiting out" a price adjustment) will need to shift gears suddenly and unexpectedly. Also, while having entered into market commitments on expectations that prove too bearish is in a sense analogous to having entered into commitments on expectations that prove too bullish, the manifestations of these two deviations from equilibrium are different. In the one case the most difficult phase is that during which the deflationary process *lasts* and in the other case that during which the inflationary process *is brought to an end*.

3. The Alleged Real-Wage Equilibrating Effect of Inflation

It bears repetition that a misconception is involved in attributing to Keynes the view that the general price level remains constant up to the capacity level of output. If this were the position held in the *General Theory*, the position would have to be rejected for the simple reason that in reality the inflation problem does acquire significance in a wide region in which Keynes disregarded it.

Yet the *General Theory* tells us that as expansionary demand-management policies move the economy from underemployment to full employment—or from a path involving lower to one involving higher employment—the general price level increases. It tells us that at a given money-wage rate this increase in the general price level leads to a reduction of the real-wage rate, thereby making real wages compatible with the requirements of fuller employment. Keynes made his position on this quite clear (see, for example, [27], the italicized passages on pp. 15 and 277). The presentation in the *General Theory* leaves one uncertain whether (1) workers allow themselves to be misled by unexpected price increases without this leading to a sequence of events that will disequilibrate the economy, or (2) they deliberately accept lower real-wage rates when the employment level is rising and the labor market is becoming tighter. The second of these suggestions would be exceedingly unconvincing. The first makes sense only for sudden one-time price increases to which the principle of "bygones are bygones" might be applicable. Continued or repetitive price increases that are unexpected—or are of unexpected steepness—cannot be generated without destabilization of the economy.

Keynes argued rightly that from labor's point of view the disadvantages of money-wage reductions are more numerous than those of a general real-wage reduction through rising prices, and that money-wage reductions are apt to have a particularly severe adverse effect on the employment level. Money-wage cuts come piecemeal in the various sectors of the economy, thereby upsetting the real-wage *structure* which in the event of the assumed *general* real-wage adjustment would call for no change. Not only do such piecemeal cuts evoke particularly strong union resistance for institutional reasons, but they also create in workers the belief that better terms of employment may be available if they quit their present jobs or insist on wage demands that will lead to layoffs. Nevertheless, it surely does not follow from this that general real-wage reductions by means of price increases are acceptable in tightening labor markets or in labor markets that are kept tight continuously. After all, real-wage reductions are unwelcome enough to workers even when the reductions are not accompanied by the special *wage-structure* effects of piecemeal money-wage cuts.

Neo-Keynesian hypotheses about the effect of inflation on real wages create serious difficulties of interpretation which are not identical with but are similar to those arising in connection with the original Keynesian hypothesis. In particular, the difficulties connected with the hypotheses of a long-run Phillips trade-off between unemployment and the rate of money-wage or price increase are not identical with the difficulties discussed above, because that hypothesis does not necessarily imply that the real wage acceptable to labor is lowered when labor markets are becoming tighter.[3] This assumption is made here only for circumstances in which the productivity of labor is adversely affected by a rise in the employment level. But what is generally implied in the hypothesis of the long-run Phillips trade-off is labor's willingness to accept at a higher level of

---

[3] The "trade-off" between inflation and unemployment has been named for A. W. Phillips because he investigated the statistical record on the relationship between the rate of unemployment and changes in money-wage rates [39]. The statistical record on a correlation between unemployment and rising prices had been explored also by Irving Fisher at an earlier date [10]. However, neither of these authors developed from their explorations the conclusion that there existed a long-run (stable) relationship between the variables—a relationship on which policy could be built. The characteristic feature of more recent work providing an argument for trading off inflation against unemployment in the long run is the claim that at given levels of unemployment (or, more generally, of labor market tightness) the corresponding inflation rate becomes gradually stabilized, with an inverse relationship between the unemployment rate and the rate of inflation. A great deal of econometric work has been devoted to this subject. See particularly [6, 18, 37].

employment the real-wage rate resulting from a higher money-wage rate and a higher inflation rate, even though this same *real* wage would not be accepted at the higher employment level in noninflationary circumstances (and thus at money wages that do not have to include compensation for inflation). What reason is there for accepting this hypothesis?

Tobin argued that the supply function of labor does indeed have the property implied in the Phillips-curve hypothesis because of intersectoral shifts within the economy, and because the money-wage steepening effect of these shifts in the favored sectors is greater than the money-wage moderating effect in the disadvantaged sectors [49]. To this asymmetry of *sectoral* wage effects there corresponds an upward trend of the price level that must be accommodated by demand management policy, provided the policy is aiming for satisfactory activity levels at which intersectoral shifts do occur and at which therefore the money-wage asymmetry must be expected to develop. Without such accommodation, Tobin argues, the relative money-wage and real-wage positions of the workers would be unacceptable to them. This argument relates not to needed changes of the general level of real wages but to needed adjustments of the wage *structure*.

Yet there are only two reasons that could explain the money-wage asymmetry in question, and neither of these justifies inflationary demand policies. The money-wage asymmetry between favored and disadvantaged sectors could develop in response to inflationary policies and, in this case, it would merely reflect these (or, what is essentially the same thing, it could reflect the realistic anticipation of such policies). The level of activity could then be kept just as high without inflationary accommodation as with it. If it cannot be kept just as high—which is the other possibility and is implied in the argument we are considering—then the asymmetry develops because real-income claims in the various sectors have become incompatible with each other at the high activity levels in question. In this case, all that could be accomplished by generating inflation would be to cover up the inconsistencies temporarily: the cover-up could last as long as increasingly expansionary demand management kept the actual inflation rate running ahead of the accelerating expected rate of inflation and allowed the real-wage structure of each successive phase of the process to differ from what was expected. This clearly involves destabilizing the system.

The logical underpinnings of the initial Keynesian hypothesis of inflationary real-wage moderation are weak indeed. So are those of the long-run Phillips trade-off that implies a more complex counterpart of the initial Keynesian hypothesis. This counterpart suggests the acceptability to labor of specific real-wage rates under inflation, though the identical real wages would not be acceptable in response to noninflationary demand management.

4. The Phillips Trade-Off in View of the American Experience

A policy based on the idea that lower unemployment-rate targets can be achieved by accepting more inflation must assume that the trade-off between inflation and unemployment exists over a sufficiently long period to justify such a policy. No one doubts that by generating unexpected inflation, and thus leading the public to overestimate the real income corresponding to its money income, it is possible to stimulate the economy temporarily, albeit at the cost of subsequent major difficulties.

A mere look at the data certainly does not give the impression that such a trade-off existed during our recent inflationary period beginning about 1965. Figure 2 plots the rate of increase of the deflator applicable to personal consumption expenditures against the measured unemployment rate in the United States; Figure 3 plots the increase in the same price measure against an unemployment rate weighted in such a way as to keep the weights of major age-sex groups in the labor force constant. Selecting the consumer price index (CPI) as the relevant price measure, or exploring the relation by plotting money-wage increases (rather than price increases) against unemployment, would leave the impression one gets essentially unchanged.

Within each of three successive subperiods the data temporarily shaped up in accordance with the trade-off hypothesis, but

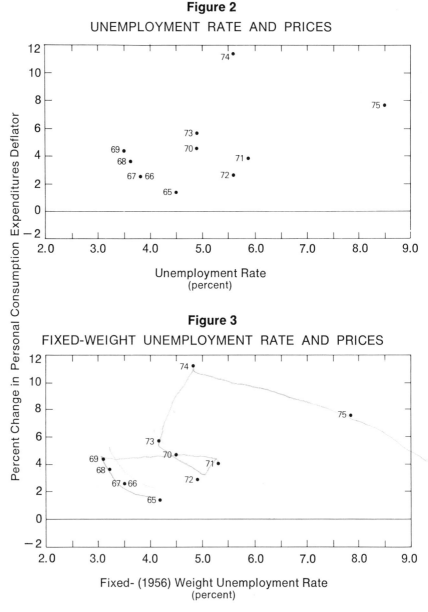

Figure 2

UNEMPLOYMENT RATE AND PRICES

Figure 3

FIXED-WEIGHT UNEMPLOYMENT RATE AND PRICES

Fixed- (1956) Weight Unemployment Rate
(percent)

Note: Wage and price controls were in effect January 1951-February 1953 and August 1971-April 1974. During these periods, however, the controls varied in comprehensiveness.

Source: Reprinted, with the omission of the pre-1965 data and with figures for 1975 added, from Council of Economic Advisers, *Annual Report* (Washington, D. C.: Government Printing Office, January 1975).

the inflation and unemployment levels at which this was happening were shifting strongly toward higher inflation *and* higher unemployment. In the last two or three years specific material-cost increases further worsened the outcome, but even in 1973 the 11.5 percent increase in money GNP would in itself have been sufficient to explain steep inflation at about 5 percent unemployment.

When a crude examination of the data produces results that are as thoroughly disappointing for a hypothesis as is the case here, it is understandable that economists would tend to explore whether more complex versions of the hypothesis lead to better results. But such a tendency is easily understandable only if the logical underpinnings of the hypothesis are solid. In the preceding section we saw how weak are the logical underpinnings of the long-run Phillips trade-off hypothesis, and yet the amount of work that has gone into constructing models of substantial complexity for validating the hypothesis has nevertheless been exceedingly large. To me this is one of the most telling symptoms of the influence of the weakest link in the Keynesian chain of reasoning, the link incorporating the equilibrating effect of a rising general price level.

The story of technically advanced work for validating the hypothesis of the trade-off can be told in brief. Models have been constructed again and again in which a number of variables jointly "explained" the observed money-wage or price increases of a past period, the unemployment rate or its reciprocal being one of these variables and this particular variable showing the effect on the inflation rate suggested by the hypothesis of the long-run Phillips trade-off. Appropriate lags have been incorporated in the models, and price expectations have been represented as a function of past price behavior. Usually the measured unemployment rate has not been used in its raw form but with allowance for the fact that the same measured overall rate can correspond to different degrees of labor market tightness. It turned out that a good many ways of setting up models of this sort gave "good results" for past periods. In the models the inflation rate was negatively correlated with the variable representing the unemployment rate, or positively correlated with its reciprocal, and the relevant coefficients were statistically significant. The models suggested that for a given level of labor market tightness the system would gradually settle down at some given inflation rate—at a higher inflation rate for lower than for higher unemployment.

Some of us were skeptical about these results from the outset because the logical foundations of the long-run trade-off hypothesis are so weak. Moreover, while the price-expectations proxies incorporated into the models rightly suggested that inflationary expectations had lagged behind reality, they seemed unsuitable for reproducing the expectational system with anything like the quantitative precision implied in the conclusions [8]. Our skepticism has been strengthened by the fact that alternative ways of arriving at "Phillips-curve" results have had implications that differed significantly on *how* the process was supposed to work. The main fact to be stressed, however, is that none of these models have so far proved adequate tools for predicting future relations between inflation and unemployment. What the untutored eye sees in Figures 2 and 3 makes much more sense than any method of explaining the result away.

5. Trends in Real Wages and in Real Profits during the Recent Inflationary Period

To any observer living in the United States it was quite clear during the decade 1965–1974 that future inflation rates were being significantly underestimated and future real incomes thus were significantly overestimated. The same fact is disclosed by opinion surveys. For example, the Survey Research Center of the University of Michigan found that even in the fall of 1973 a large proportion of their respondents expected a moderate rate of inflation for the coming twelve months. As many as 87 percent expected less than the double-digit inflation that actually occurred, and the bulk of these underestimated future inflation by a significant margin.

As for the statistical record, during the first half of the inflationary period 1965–1974—that is, from 1965 to 1969—real compensation per man-hour in the private nonfarm sector rose at an annual compound rate of 2.5 percent, the same rate as in the preceding noninflationary eight-year period, 1957–1965. This increase occurred in spite of the fact that productivity trends had weakened significantly by 1965–1969. Inflation performed no real-wage-moderating function at that time.

Subsequently, productivity trends were further weakened, and in the second half of the inflationary span 1965–1974—that is, from 1969 to 1974—actual real compensation per man-hour rose less than it had in the noninflationary eight-year period, 1957–1965: from 1969 to 1974 the annual compound rate of increase was only 1.2 percent, some 1.3 percentage points lower than the rate of increase from 1957 to 1965. A one percentage point difference (hence a similar difference) shows in the same direction between 1969–1974 and 1957–1965 when we consider real adjusted hourly earnings in the private nonfarm sector instead of considering real compensation per man-hour.[4] But 1969–1974 was a period in which there were two real-wage-moderating recessions and during which the terms of trade shifted against the country at large and against the nonfarm sector in particular. These facts alone cast strong doubts on any real-wage-moderating effect that could be attributed to inflation in the latter period.

Furthermore, any reasonable estimate of what the expected increase of real compensation or in real adjusted hourly earnings may have been from 1969 to 1974—the rate expected, that is, when account is taken of the underestimate of the impending inflation rates—must suggest that the expected rise of 1969–1974 (when compared to the actual increase of 1957–1965) showed a smaller shortfall than is suggested by the numbers just cited and may well have shown no shortfall at all. The "expected average annual rise" in adjusted hourly earnings (though not in real compensation) in the inflationary period 1969–1974 was

---

[4] In contrast to real compensation, real adjusted hourly earnings contain an adjustment for interindustry shifts and, in the manufacturing industries, also for overtime; on the other hand, they do not include fringe benefits.

practically the same as the actual increase in the noninflationary period 1957–1965 if we construct a very imprecise but suggestive "proxy" for the expected rise by correcting the nominal increase of each current year by the price increase of the preceding year rather than by the price increase of the current year (which was unknown at the time commitments were entered into).[5] This conclusion holds for the five-year period 1969–1974 in spite of the two real-wage-moderating recessions and the adverse terms-of-trade effects of these latter years. Both recessions of the period 1969–1974—that of 1969–1970 and that of 1973–1975 —occurred at a time when the authorities tried to put an end to a rapidly accelerating inflationary process, and the second of the two raised the measured unemployment rate temporarily into the 8 to 9 percent range.

There are no signs in these data of a real-wage equilibrating effect of inflation, or of any inflation effect that would have promoted the acceptability of real-wage reductions relative to the trend. There are strong signs that real-wage movements moderated during periods of slackened activity, especially periods in which the slackening coincided with adverse changes of the country's international terms of trade or with changes in the industrial sector's terms of trade with the farm sector (or with both). During the recession of 1973–1975 this expressed itself in an outright reduction of actually earned real-wage rates. At the same time, the available information strongly suggests that expected real-wage rates were higher than those actually earned because of an underestimate on the part of labor of future inflation—a destabilizing factor.

While for our present purpose there exists no entirely satisfactory way of defining profit trends, it seems likely that real profits were significantly overestimated during the post-1965 period, and that their overestimation came partly from inadequately appraising the consequences of the accelerating inflation rate. From 1965 to 1973 the *gross* book profits of all nonfinancial corporations, deducting neither taxes nor depreciation charges,

---

[5] For adjusted hourly earnings the arithmetic mean of these "expected increases" was 1.8 percent for 1969-1974, while the actual compound rate of increase was 1.9 percent for 1957-1965.

rose by about 17 percent when these gross book profits are deflated for price changes. The deflated sum of these "gross profits" and of net interest or borrowed capital rose by about 25 percent, while the best estimate for the country's stock of nonresidential fixed business capital points to a 45 percent increase of this stock as valued in constant prices.[6]

On the assumption that a general underestimate of the impending inflation led to the payment of lower real wages than had been expected either by workers or their employers, the disappointing profit trend of the period should presumably be interpreted as a result of a pronounced weakening of the productivity trend (to be shown in Table 1 below) and of a deterioration of the nonfarm sector's domestic and international terms of trade. To what extent these adverse circumstances are to be regarded as specific characteristics of the period under consideration and to what extent as results of inflation in general is debatable; yet it is difficult to conceive of an accelerating inflationary movement that will not lead to a significant deterioration of the productivity performance, if no earlier than by the time when the inevitable effort is made to end the movement.

Any reasonable common-sense appraisal suggests that the post-1965 inflation provided a temporary economic stimulus by misleading the public concerning available real incomes. This purely short-run gain—exploitation of a short-run trade-off between inflation and unemployment—was associated with a subsequent setback of major dimensions.

6. The Uselessness of the Distinction between Voluntary and Involuntary Unemployment

Ever since the publication of the *General Theory* the idea of involuntary unemployment has caused significant analytical difficulties. Keynes's definition is unhelpful, and so are all variants inspired by that definition. But this does not matter much, because the relevant pragmatic question for demand manage-

---

[6] The 45 percent estimate is based on the same data that will be described in Chapter IV, Section 3, and will be used in Table 2 in that section.

ment policy is *not* how many nonworking persons aged sixteen years or over are without a job "voluntarily" and how many are without a job "involuntarily." The relevant question is rather this: how many will have a job and how many will not if demand management policy promotes the maximum amount of employment that can be achieved over a reasonable time period without reliance on a destabilizing inflationary process?

Keynes tried to define involuntary unemployment as that unemployment which can be eliminated by expansionary demand policies, as did Tobin in a neo-Keynesian vein. Both Keynes and Tobin reject a test of involuntariness which would require that those qualifying as involuntarily unemployed should be willing to offer their services at reduced money-wage rates. Keynes proposed that involuntariness of unemployment be interpreted as expressing itself in willingness to accept a job at reduced real-wage rates in the event that the real-wage reduction resulted from price increases brought about by expansionary demand policy [27, p. 15]. Tobin [48] suggested modifying this definition and adapting it to growth economics by requiring of the "involuntarily" unemployed that *in response to expansionary policies* they should be willing to accept jobs at real-wage rates compatible with the additional employment. Acceptance of these real-wage rates need not necessarily involve a moderation of the economy's usual real-wage trend. Yet, as we have seen, Tobin, like Keynes, suggests that an appropriate demand policy needs to accommodate a rising price trend. He arrives at this conclusion by arguing that, in an economy in which intersectoral shifts are taking place, a higher employment level will be compatible with acceptable money and real wages if the asymmetry between money-wage movements in favored and disadvantaged sectors is accommodated in this way. We have found the initial Keynesian hypothesis of inflationary real-wage equilibration unconvincing and have arrived at the same conclusion about neo-Keynesian adaptations of the hypothesis. In general, all concepts of involuntary unemployment that aim for analytical precision hinge on hypotheses it is advisable to avoid.

The distinction between voluntary and involuntary unemployment is analytically valid in strictly defined perfectly competitive neoclassical equilibrium. Even there the distinction is valid only in the sense that the definitional properties of that state assure the *nonexistence* of involuntary unemployment, that is, the voluntary character of all remaining unemployment. No useful purpose would, however, be served by defining the involuntary component as the difference between the actually observed unemployment and that which would exist in perfectly competitive equilibrium.

Skepticism about useful criteria for the distinction sometimes focuses on the ambiguities that arise from union action preventing a downward adjustment of wages to the requirements of higher employment at a time when the individual workers would be willing to adjust their wage demands downward. In Chapter VII it will be argued that the difficulties of drawing the distinction are much more deep-rooted than this, and that in very few cases is it possible even to make sense of the question how elements of voluntariness and of involuntariness are mixed together for the persons included in our unemployment statistics. A policy aiming for the maximum sustainable activity level need not, however, concern itself with this unanswerable question.

7. Employment Policy and Alternative Price-Level Targets

Concern with price level targets to which market expectations can be conditioned must be supplemented by concern with employment policy objectives whenever a *range* of activity levels is compatible with the price level targets. Given such a range, a "price-level oriented" demand policy has good reason to aim for the upper end. It will be explained in Chapter IV why such ranges may well exist even in the neighborhood of a normal growth path. Their existence is the reason we are not building into this analysis the concept of the "natural rate of unemployment" [13], to which the actual rate is supposed to move in the long run regardless of demand management policy. The "natural rate of unemployment" is a legitimate concept only in a system tending to full neoclassical competitive equilibrium. It cannot be adjusted to given "actual characteristics of the labor and commodity markets," as Friedman asks us to do.[7] Nor does Friedman in practice suggest basing policy on the theory that the natural rate of unemployment will be established regardless of demand management: on the contrary, he advocates a policy of adopting money-growth targets that he expects to be compatible with sustainable price-level behavior.

A price-level-oriented demand policy would have to remain aware of employment policy objectives even if the authorities were concerned only with the "long run." Moreover, shorter-run considerations, of course, also matter if they complement rather than displace consideration relating to the longer run. In circumstances where the price trend is not yet out of hand to such an extent that a gradual approach to a sustainable price-level behavior would have become unpromising, consistently adopted gradualism may avoid the kind of shock that could cause very large temporary unemployment. But because, even in the event of gradualism, the characteristics of a transition period depend on the price level target chosen, this raises a question we have so far avoided. After a period of accelerating inflation, to what kind of behavior should a reasonable demand-management policy attempt to condition market expectations? From our analysis it does not follow on purely logical grounds that the objective must be to establish a practically horizontal price trend. Much can be said for choosing this objective, but that choice does not follow from economic analysis with the same cogency as does the requirement of establishing reasonably predictable price-level behavior *of some sort* in an approach to macroeconomic equilibrium. An effort could be made to gear the expectational system to a steady upward trend of the price level or to a steady downward trend. In either case, the tax system would have to be adjusted in such a way that the increments being taxed be defined with correction for price changes.

A steady upward trend of the price level would penalize non-interest-bearing liquid assets, including currency, and would thus set a premium on the ownership of other assets. No reason-

---

[7] Phelps, after deriving his concept of the natural rate of unemployment from the main part of his analysis, adds a qualifying remark which recognizes a difficulty related to that stressed here [38].

able case could be made for the implied "tax-subsidy" scheme as such. All that could be argued in favor of a steady uptrend is that, with the inflation rates now observable in the Western world as the point of departure, to stabilize (say) a 5 percent steady inflation rate would involve a shorter period of substantial demand-policy restraint than to establish near-zero rates of inflation. On the other hand, commitment to a steady appreciable price uptrend would probably have little credibility. Inasmuch as such a policy would start by not considering the restoration of noninflationary conditions worth the effort, it would surely be expected not to consider the difference between 6 and 5 percent, and thereafter between 7 and 6 percent, and so on, worth the effort in the future. Market expectations cannot be conditioned by a policy that lacks credibility.

If we seek guidance from the axiomatic system of technical welfare economics, a better case could be made for a steady downtrend of the price level. This would be one possible method of securing for the holders of non-interest-bearing liquid assets a *real rate of return* corresponding to the time preference of savers. As Friedman has explained [12], the case for the steady downtrend rests on the fact that the owners of the assets in question are increasing the availability of consumer goods to others. However, as Friedman has also explained, it is impossible to derive a good quantitative estimate of the rate of return—that is, of the rate of decline of the price level—that would be justified by these criteria. Quite generally, it is difficult to appraise the advisability of trying to live up to the requirements of an axiomatic system in one specific area, when it would be clearly impossible to organize a large number of other areas by the same principles. This is a general weakness of normative propositions derived from technical welfare economics. The case for making such an effort with price trends is particularly shaky because of the high degree of imprecision of the quantitative estimates on which the effort would necessarily be based.

We conclude that a strong case can be made for regarding a horizontal price trend as the target to be approached, even if the argument favoring the choice of that target does not have the general analytical validity of the argument leading to the conclusion that the price level must be correctly foreseen in a state of macro-equilibrium.

8. Success and Failure in Past Periods

If followed through consistently, a gradual approach to a sustainable behavior of the price level would have a good chance of proving successful. For the reasons explained in Chapter I, private decision makers individually contemplating a behavior inconsistent with the required typical behavior would know in advance that it would be too costly for them to follow such behavior. They would know this no matter whether they assumed that for the time being others would also develop that kind of behavior or assumed that most others would fall in line with the policy objectives. This is how it worked during periods in which major and sustained deviations from "usual" price-level behavior were prevented, either after major inflationary interludes or without immediate antecedents of that sort. To be sure, what was credible to the public in the more distant past was not so much a clearly formulated price-level objective on the part of the authorities as a set of institutional constraints. Determination to adhere to a system of fixed exchange rates based on the gold standard in a like-minded international community introduced such a constraint. This was rightly expected to be incompatible with significantly inflationary policies, while making it usually (though not always) possible to compensate for major deflationary tendencies. Such a system would not work in the present international environment. Nevertheless, in the postwar era we did have a period of fair duration in which the American authorities were in fact credible in their effort to achieve practical stability of the price level, and this cannot be attributed to constraints comparable to those imposed by the gold standard in the more distant past. The Bretton Woods system did not provide comparable safeguards against consistent inflationary trends.

The question now is whether monetary and fiscal policies not subject to constraints other than those accepted ad hoc by legislative bodies and central banks can credibly be directed at price level objectives compatible with reasonably stable growth. The method of achieving this would necessarily have to be that of generating an aggregate nominal demand coming near to absorbing the highest output judged compatible with the price level objective to which the economy is geared. Monetary growth and fiscal targets are necessary for achieving this objective, though these targets must be sufficiently adjustable not to render the price level target adjustable instead, and thereby ineffective.

Doubts are likely to arise in the minds of the public about the promise of these techniques because the decision to limit oneself to techniques that are very mild when compared to those employed in rigorously controlled societies has often shaded over into indecision and into failure. It is not easy to make it understood that losing the "game of strategy" that inevitably develops between the authorities and the public would, after a few rounds, bring gains to no more than a very small number of winners and would cause great losses to the bulk of the population. Yet, before going too far in this kind of skepticism it is advisable for us to take a look at the characteristics of a period that does not lie far back in the past, and wherein the strategy of the American authorities did in fact yield reasonably satisfactory results. It will be shown later in this volume that, so far as they concern the variables a successful demand policy would have to watch, our oft-maligned forecasting methods have stood up better recently than in earlier years. The same general line of policy could therefore now become more successful than it was then in the avoidance of economic fluctuations. This is true all the more because the demand restraints that contributed to the last of the three recessions of our postwar period of price stability were mainly motivated not by price level objectives but by the objective of ensuring the convertibility of the dollar into gold.[8] This, however, was merely a brief episode: neither before nor after it were our demand policies shaped with such a constraint in mind.

---

[8] This relates to the recession of 1960-1961. The preceding recessions of that period were those of 1953-1954 and 1957-1958.

The period of a stable price trend extended from the early 1950s to the mid-1960s. The general record of that period will be contrasted here with the record of the following decade, and comments will be added on the break in policy attitudes between the years of price stability and the years that followed. In Chapter VII the nature of these policies will be further explored in a discussion of possible future courses for the United States authorities.

We turn to the data presented in Table 1, noting that our compound rates involve continuous compounding.

Table 1

PRICE MOVEMENTS, UNEMPLOYMENT RATES, AND SOME OTHER INDICATORS OF PERFORMANCE, IN PERCENT, 1951–1975

		Annual Compound Rates of Change from First to Last Year of Period			
			Private nonfarm sector		
Period	CPI	GNP deflator	Real compensation per man-hour	Output per man-hour	Period's Average Unemployment Rate[a]
Five-year or Shorter Periods					
1951–55	0.8	1.6	3.5	2.3	3.8
1955–60	2.0	2.4	2.7	1.8	5.2
1960–65	1.3	1.6	2.5	3.2	5.5 (in 1965: 4.5)
1965–69	3.8	3.9	2.5	1.7	3.7
1969–72	4.4	4.7	2.0	2.5	5.5
1972–73	6.0	5.8	1.5	2.0	4.9
1973–74	10.4	9.3	− 1.3	− 2.4	5.6
1974–75	8.7	8.4	− 0.2	0.9	8.5
Eight-year or Longer Periods					
1951–65	1.4	1.9	2.9	2.5	4.9
1957–65	1.4	1.7	2.5	2.9	5.5
1965–73	4.3	4.4	2.2	2.0	4.5
1965–74	5.0	5.0	1.8	1.5	4.6
1965–75	5.3	5.3	1.6	1.5	5.0

[a] With the exception of 1951 and 1957, all "first years" of the spans were excluded from the averaging in this column, to avoid inclusion in two successive spans.

The period from 1951 through 1965 was one of practical stability of the general price level. Moreover, during those fourteen years the "all commodities" component of the consumer price index (CPI) rose at an average annual rate of only 0.8 percent, and in an economy with rising real-wage rates one would expect the service component to show a greater increase than is shown by the commodities components. During that period the unemployment rate had a rising tendency. In the proper interpretation of this tendency, the "Perry shift" [37] in the composition of the civilian labor force deserves emphasis, though not to the exclusion of other considerations.

From the beginning to the end of the period 1951–1965 the representation of adult males (aged twenty and over) in the civilian labor force declined from 65.6 to 60.2 percent, and that of males aged twenty-five to sixty-four from 55.2 to 50.7 percent. The representation of adult females rose from 27.8 to 31.8 percent, and that of teenagers of both sexes from 6.6 to 7.9 percent. Adult women have higher unemployment rates than adult men, as measured by our sampling survey method, because there are relatively more entrants and reentrants into the labor force among them, and normally the decision to enter or to reenter precedes a job offer and the decision to accept it. This seems to be the sole explanation of the higher unemployment rate of adult women, if we judge by the fact that if entrants and reentrants are excluded, then in the six years from 1969 to 1974 they had an unemployment rate of 2.8 percent, as against the corresponding male rate of 2.7 percent (see [3], p. 103). The relatively high unemployment rate of teenagers and of the age class twenty through twenty-four is also explained in part by the higher proportion of entrants and reentrants in those groups than among males aged twenty-five and beyond. Yet, for those in the young categories we need also to take account of their less steady attachment to a given job while they remain in the labor force. At any rate, there occurred during the period from 1951 through 1965 a significant increase in the labor force representation of workers whose specific unemployment rate was appreciably higher than that of the groups whose representation was declining. This fact possesses obvious significance in ex-

61

plaining the rising trend in unemployment during the period, particularly because the unemployment rate for married men was the same in 1964–1965 as it had been in the mid-1950s.

A more complete analysis would also have to take account of other changes—such as the rising level of education and the blue-collar to white-collar shift. Considered by themselves, these changes might have been expected to reduce the unemployment rate. But the Perry shift in labor force composition was doubtless a strong unemployment-raising factor that would have left its mark on the trends in any event, even though better foresight by the policy makers would have reduced the cyclical fluctuations of the period. The shift in the composition in the labor force has continued at a significant rate after 1965.[9]

The price performance up to 1965 showed no signs of a policy effort to use inflationary techniques for preventing the rise in the overall unemployment rate. Market expectations must have become reasonably well conditioned to the stability of the price level, though by the early part of the 1960s strong political criticism of the unemployment trend may have started raising doubts whether a change were not in the offing.

With the periods constructed as they are in Table 1, a rather sharp demand-policy break is suggested for the mid-1960s. It will be seen later that this suggestion is basically correct. Cagan used a method by which it is possible to observe signs of a gradually worsening price performance even during the 1950s, in the sense that the price-trend moderating effect of successive recessions (as dated by the National Bureau of Economic Research) tended to become weaker [2]. Of course the price level performance of a longer period as a whole depends not only on this but also on the behavior during the preceding expansion. The period from 1951 through 1965 started and ended during the expansion phase of a cycle, with three peaks and troughs located between the first and the last year of the period.

The record started to differ significantly after 1965, as will be evident from a look at the entries in the table for the essential

---

[9] By 1975 the representation of adult men in the civilian labor force had declined to 54.9 percent, the representation of adult women had risen to 35.6 percent, and that of teenagers of both sexes to 9.5 percent.

subperiod 1965–1969. In these four years—to be precise, in the four-year interval that followed the *fiscal* year 1965—the Vietnam War raised defense expenditures by 65 percent (about $30 billion), while at the same time the nondefense expenditures of the federal government rose by 49 percent (about $35 billion). The large rise in nondefense expenditures was caused by a steep increase in government transfer payments, the rapid rise of which continued after the close of the four-year subperiod. What is relevant to the interpretation of the break in the price performance is not this fact but the methods of financing all these expenditures. To this problem of changing policy attitudes we shall return in Chapter VII. Before we do so, we shall examine some of the essential properties of growth paths in whose neighborhood appropriate demand management should be able to keep us more successfully than in the past.

IV

Induced Innovations, Distributive Shares, and Sustainable Employment along the Growth Path

1. Rates of Return and Distributive Shares

To fit the kind of macro-equilibrium Keynes attempted to formalize into the context of economic growth calls for tying successive short periods in with one another. Hardly had the *General Theory* been published when these analytical tying-in operations started. Without going into details of alternative ways of formalizing the results, we may describe them with reference to Figure 4.

The arrows show the period-to-period upward shift of output along a growth path. The points marked on the individual curves represent macro-equilibria in which the economy would settle down were it not for the acquisition of additional resources (labor and capital) and for technological advance. We are implying that along each curve a higher labor input is associated with a higher capital input in the same proportion. The curvature to the right of the straight stretches is intended to express the shift in the composition of the employed toward lower-productivity workers at high employment levels, and also to express the fact that the assumption of equiproportionate resource increases cannot be upheld for natural resources of equal quality beyond some point. We now turn to the growth path.

The constancy of the horizontal distance of all points of the growth path from the origin is an unessential simplifying assumption. Note that 100 less the percentage measured along the

Figure 4

SKETCH OF A NORMAL GROWTH PATH

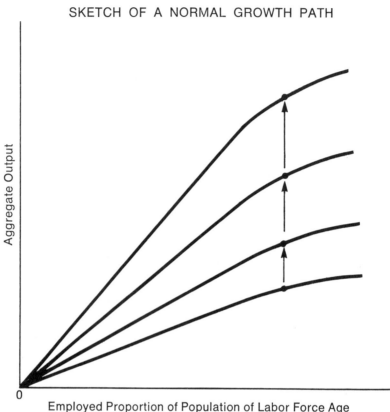

Aggregate Output

0

Employed Proportion of Population of Labor Force Age

Legend: Each curve applies to a single period. The arrows show the upward shift over time along the growth path, given the employment ratio.

horizontal axis is *not* what is called the unemployment rate: the unemployment rate is defined as a percentage of the civilian labor force, not of the labor-force-age population. For our present purpose it is preferable to label the abscissa this way because, given any unemployment rate, a change in the labor force participation rate affects the employment level (as would, of course, a change in the unemployment rate given the participation rate). In the United States, over the past twenty-five years the participation rate has been moving between 60 and 62 percent, with the rate for men declining and that for women rising.

In an economy in which part of the net product consists of investment goods, output must be rising from period to period if the investments are to be justified (profitable). Furthermore, so long as the public does not increase its consumption by the entire addition to output developing along the time path, the absolute amount of investment must increase, unless a rise in government expenditures on goods and services takes up the difference between output growth and the growth of consumption. Normally we find an increase of both consumption and investment along the growth path. For the rate of return on investment not to decline in spite of the growth of the capital stock, either resources other than capital must be increasing in a proportion no smaller than that in which capital is growing or there must be technological progress that maintains the yield of capital even though relative to capital the resources cooperating with it are becoming scarcer on the growth path.

In Western developed economies the resources other than capital have typically been rising in a much lesser proportion than the capital stock. Any reasonable interpretation of the trends that have emerged in developed economies in these circumstances must place considerable emphasis on technological progress brought about by the acquisition of new skills. Apart from technological advance, rates of return on investment would have declined significantly, and while we do have indications of a declining profit-rate tendency not limited to recent years of relatively poor economic performance, there has been no secular shrinkage of "real" yields such as one would expect to observe in a world in which the capital stock has for a long time risen in a much higher proportion than other inputs. Long-run trends direct attention to technological advance. Technological advance in turn requires inventiveness and risk taking, and it therefore also requires an environment conducive to the latter.

If rates of return on investment did decline to very low levels, and the risks of investment prevented the channelling into capital formation of the savings developing at a given level of employment, this could have one of three consequences. We may describe the first possible consequence as a validation of Say's Law by the emergence of a deflationary real-balance effect, producing an increase of the real value of liquid assets sufficient to induce the consumption demand required for maintaining the previous employment level. Given the difficulties of this kind of adjustment process we should, however, concentrate not on this consequence but on one of the remaining two. One of these would be a reduction of savings as a result of a reduction of output and of the employment level. The other would be a significant increase of deficit-financed government expenditures, made either on goods and services directly or as disbursements to households in the form of consumption-raising transfer payments. In circumstances in which investment opportunities would have been reduced by diminishing returns to capital to such an extent that even at very low interest rates too little investment would be forthcoming to match savings at otherwise sustainable activity levels (describing Keynes's "liquidity trap"), a strong case could be made for offsetting the high-employment savings by large government deficits. These deficits would represent dissaving by the government at high activity levels, and it would be more desirable to reduce the aggregate of private and public saving in this fashion than to allow the activity level to shrink to a point where private savings would be eliminated or greatly reduced.[1]

---

[1] To see in what sense the government deficit needs to be deducted from private savings—that is, represents dissaving—consider the basic macroeconomic accounting identity:

Consumption + Private Domestic Investment + Investment Abroad
+ Government Expenditures on Goods and Services = Consumption
+ Private Savings + Tax Payments − Government Transfer Payments.

Both sides of the equation equal the value of aggregate output. Now omit consumption from both sides, and carry the last item on the left-hand side over to the right-hand side. The accounting identity then requires that domestic investment added to the country's investments abroad should be equal to private savings less the government deficit. This being clearly the correct form of the savings-investment identity when the government is included, it follows that the government deficit is an item of deduction from private savings (that is to say, plays the role of dissavings).

The country's investment abroad is equivalent to its net exports of goods and services, and from this in turn it follows that even in the Keynesian liquidity trap (where government expenditures displace no domestic investment) a government deficit has an expansionary effect only to the extent that it does not raise imports relative to exports—that is, does not diminish investment abroad. See Chapter II, Section 6.

Keynes was inclined to see a situation like this on the horizon for a not-too-distant future which, however, he described very vaguely. Yet his "stagnationist" premonitions, which at that time were further elaborated upon by his American followers, were based on a significant underestimate of the potency of technological progress within any time horizon for which it is advisable to engage in speculation. Technological progress has acted to counter the forces that would bring about a decline in the return on investment in growing economies. Moreover, the factor-saving effects of progress have been distributed among the various input categories in a way that has enabled technological progress to perform this countering function effectively.

Diminishing returns to capital as a result of a lesser proportionate increase in the inputs cooperating with capital will not lead us into secular stagnation in the foreseeable future. The critical problems of the present period were not caused by a tendency toward stagnation and the unwillingness or inability of the authorities to offset that tendency by expansionary measures. On the contrary, they were caused by overexpansion and what may be called the fooling effect of inflation.

2. Innovations and Income Distribution

The answer to the question how the real-wage rate is influenced by the growth process expressing itself in the vertical upward shift of the curves in Figure 4 depends on how the differential growth rates of the various types of input *on the one hand* and the character of technological progress *on the other hand* contribute to determining the distribution of income.

Before turning to more complex but more realistic assumptions, we shall first assume that the distribution of income remains unchanged as we move up vertically in Figure 4, no matter how rapidly the labor input is growing relative to other inputs and no matter what the rate of technological progress along the growth path so described. Such results can be derived from a Cobb-Douglas production function with neutral progress. They can be derived alternatively from constant elasticity of substitution (CES) functions with less than unitary elasticity of substitution when these are combined with labor-augmenting progress. But we shall not have to commit ourselves here to these tools when we initially assume a constant relative distribution of income for any observed change in input ratios and for any observed rate of technological advance.

On this simple assumption we may conclude that the real-wage rate will be changing in the same proportion as output per unit of labor input (Q/L). We may add that in circumstances typical of Western economies the change of Q/L along the growth path will be an increase in the ratio. It will be an increase if, when we move vertically from period to period in Figure 4, the resource inputs other than labor are rising in a higher proportion than the labor input. The change in Q/L would be an increase even if the other inputs were rising in the same proportion as the labor input and there were *any* technological progress, or even if the other inputs rose in a lesser proportion and there were *enough* technological progress. In fact, the capital stock has been rising in a higher proportion than the L input and, given the higher rate of increase of the capital stock, the real-wage rate would be rising in relation to the rate of return per unit of capital. This would hold *even* on the simplifying assumption so far made that relative shares in the aggregate income or output of the economy remained constant. Even on that assumption, the given relative share of capital in income would imply a less favorable trend for income *per unit of capital employed* than the trend described for income per unit of L input.

However, the rise of the real-wage rate in relation to the rate of return on capital has been more pronounced than these statements would suggest, because the relative share of labor in output has in fact increased. Invariance of distributive shares (relative shares) in response to the joint effect of changing input ratios and technological progress—invariance, that is, when we move upward along the growth path in Figure 4—is a simplifying assumption we now need to relax. For example, for the United States we have indications that from 1948 to the present, looking at spans bordered by cyclically comparable years, there have been periods of approximately constant labor share and also periods of rising labor share, with the result that over the half-century or more the L share has increased. This raises the question whether in market economies there exist forces that keep such shifts within bounds, and this question has received a good deal of attention over the past two decades or so. The question should not, of course, be confused with the question of changes in relative shares during the business cycle—that is, with the problem of the cyclical decline of the profit share (rise of the L share) during the contraction phase of the cycle and the contrary shift during its expansion phase.

Theories of distributive shares constancy along the growth path imply highly restrictive assumptions about production functions and substitution elasticities, or slightly less restrictive assumptions about these and highly restrictive ones about so-called innovation possibility frontiers [25, 26, 42, 43]. Not only is it true that the United States data would be difficult to reconcile with the conclusions derived from these assumptions, but it is also true that the assumptions are so specific as to have raised suspicions about the foundations of that hypothesis from the outset.

I will further elaborate on a suggestion I have made in this regard since the beginning of the debate. A strong case can be made for a hypothesis that is a good deal less rigid than that of shares constancy [7, 9]. The hypothesis is that when distributive shares shift—for example, when the L share rises—the innovations assume characteristics that work in the contrary direction. Therefore, a presumption exists that shifts towards a higher labor share become suppressed or remain minor in periods in which innovating activity is running "sufficiently high" in a sense that *could* be defined in terms of neoclassical production functions, but that I shall now express without reliance on these.

3. Offsetting Tendencies

Before explaining what should be meant by a "sufficiently high" rate of innovation or of technological advance—sufficiently high for suppressing changes in relative shares—the question needs to be answered why one would expect innovations to work against a rising relative share of labor (or of some other input) in the total product. We should note first that if total costs consist of (say) 70 percent labor cost and 30 percent nonlabor cost, then *given the identical expenses and effort* it would be far more rewarding for innovators to concentrate on finding new methods by which labor input and labor costs might be reduced by X percent per unit of output than on discovering methods by which nonlabor input and nonlabor costs might be reduced in the same proportion. Hence, there is good reason to assume that with the shares at (say) 70 and 30 percent, the expenses and effort needed for reducing labor cost by X percent per unit of output are correspondingly greater than those needed for reducing the nonlabor cost per unit of output in the same proportions. If this were not so, the 70 to 30 ratio would presumably not have established itself because the innovational efforts would have been directed primarily at reducing the L costs and thus the L share in income. The share of capital (K) would have been higher.

In view of actual developments in our economies, we should now consider the change that occurs when, as a result of savings, more goods become available for capital formation but the L supply does not rise correspondingly. If innovations did not enable investors to introduce new kinds of equipment, the additional capital goods would after a short while be worth very little. Some amount of additional capital formation could take place for a while in circumstances not extremely unfavorable, because even for physically given capital goods the input proportions are not literally fixed, and also because firms employing more labor-using equipment could copy the practices of firms whose equipment is less labor-using. But a major sustained shift toward higher K/L ratios would require newly invented kinds of equipment in order to yield an appreciable addition to output. If new kinds of equipment did not become available through innovations, any sustained increase in the K/L ratio would lead to an exceedingly steep increase in wage rates and of the L share in income, and to a reduction of the capital share to an exceedingly low level. The remaining capital share would be earned on capital goods, the usefulness of which would have become very small indeed.

In these circumstances the incentive to direct innovations at the reduction of the L input per unit of output, rather than at the reduction of the K input, would be greatly strengthened. This incentive would result *inter alia* in a highly intensive search for ways of constructing less labor-using types of equipment. Whereas the difficulties (effort and expenses) of making further progress along these lines may well be increasing as the K intensity of the economy increases, the gross payoff (payoff without allowance for the innovational expenses) would become tilted exceedingly strongly in favor of reducing the L input per unit of output, rather than reducing the K input (whose supply, in the absence of innovating activity, would become an excess supply at near-zero price). If the price of K services declined to near the zero level, it would clearly be more profitable to search for innovations reducing the L input rather than the K input, even if the K-saving innovations would be much cheaper to come by.

The hypothesis based on these considerations can be developed in the following steps: (1) For a given path of L inputs, innovations have the macroeconomic effect of raising the Q/L ratio. (2) When the K/L ratio rises significantly, one of the essential functions of innovating activity is to enable the economy to raise Q/L by putting additional K inputs to productive use with reliance on newly invented kinds of equipment. (3) By performing this function, innovating activity leads to a steeper increase in Q/L than the increase that could develop with unchanging kinds of capital goods. (4) Also by performing this same function, innovating activity prevents the extreme reduction of the K share, and it prevents the corresponding extreme increase in the L share, that would take place if the savings accruing in the economy were incorporated into unchanging kinds of additional equipment. (5) Thus—in view of (3) and (4)—the presumption is created that when, given any rate of increase of K/L along the growth path, the Q/L ratio rises significantly—that is, the economy proves capable of making good use of the additional K input—the level of innovating activity is much more likely to be "sufficiently high" for preventing a rise in the L share than it is when the rise in Q/L is small in relation to that in K/L. If the rise in Q/L is small in relation to that in K/L, innovating activity is too weak to achieve shares stabilization. In this case the economy does not become sufficiently well endowed with the new kinds of capital goods required for putting the additional K input to highly productive use. This is our hypothesis.

The process here outlined makes the increase in Q/L a proxy for innovations, and the nearest we get to testing our hypothesis is by exploring whether along our growth path there has tended to be a lesser increase in the L share when there has occurred a greater increase in Q/L per unit increase of K/L than when there has occurred little increase in Q/L as compared to the increase in K/L. A number of difficulties are involved in making such a test more than suggestive, not the least of these being the fact that all measures of the aggregate real capital stock are subject to uncertainties, including conceptual ambiguities. Even so, the outcome of the test is distinctly suggestive.

In Table 2 the L share is measured by the share of employee compensation in the privately produced national income. The L share so expressed therefore does not include the labor-income component of the income of unincorporated business (farm or nonfarm). Over the past decade these incomes, which the table fails to split into a labor and a nonlabor component, have accounted for about 8 to 12 percent of the privately produced national income, while in the early part of the period following 1948 the range had been about twice as high. The real K stock here is the Department of Commerce's "net fixed nonresident business capital stock in 1958 prices, variant 2, straight-line depreciation, 85 percent of Bulletin F service lives." The L input is the estimate by the Bureau of Labor Statistics of this input in the private economy as a whole (not only in the nonfarm economy), and the Q/L data are those for output per man-hour taken from the corresponding Bureau of Labor Statistics series. Hence, the symbols K, Q, and L do not have here the same meaning as in our general theoretical discussion of the entire economy.

Table 2
CAPITAL INTENSITY, INNOVATIONS, AND
DISTRIBUTIVE SHARES

Period (1)	Annual Compound Rate of Change (in percent)		Column 3 Divided by Column 2 (4)	Share of Employee Compensation in Privately Produced N.I., Beginning and End of Period (in percent) (5)
	K/L (2)	Q/L (3)		
1948–57	4.0	3.2	0.8	61.5–67.3
1957–60	2.5	2.7	1.1	67.3–67.9
1960–65	2.7	3.6	1.3	67.9–66.0
1965–69	3.9	2.1	0.5	66.0–70.4
1969–73	2.6	2.5	1.0	70.4–70.6

Note: To the second and fifth entry in Column 4 (which are intermediate between the high entry and the low ones) there corresponds little change in the L share; to the one higher entry in Column 4 there corresponds a decline; to the lower entries there correspond increases. The periods extend from cyclical peak year to peak year, except that a subperiod is made to end in 1965. The same conclusion would be suggested on the relation between Column 4 and Column 5 if we moved from 1960 to 1969 without a break. Separating the period 1948-1953 from the remainder of the table's first period would make a difference, because 1948-1953 would have the number 1.1 in the fourth column (practically the same as 1957-1960 and 1969-1973) and yet it would show a significant rise in Column 5, followed by a much smaller rise for 1953-1957. However, the fact that 1948-1953 begins with an extraordinary increase of 5.8 percent in real adjusted hourly earnings from 1948 to 1949 suggests that the adjustment following the World War II controls played a large role in shaping the L-share characteristics of that five-year period. If 1948-1953 is nevertheless included as a separate period, the conclusion is that between the high value in Column 4, to which there corresponds a decline in Column 5, and low values to which there correspond rises, there is in Column 4 an in-between range with an ambiguous relation to Column 5.

In an earlier study it was shown that up to 1965 the results were in all probability not affected by industry shifts [9]. Nor probably were they significantly enough affected for the years 1965–1973 to make a difference, though that test was not carried out for the most recent years. Furthermore, it is even unclear whether in the present context a correction should be made for these shifts that at least partly reflect the workings of the mechanism here hypothesized. We see that smallness of Q/L growth *relative to the increase in* K/L—the weakness of innovational effects in this sense—has described the conditions in which the L share was rising. A sufficiently large rise in Q/L relative to K/L—the strength of innovational effects in this sense—is characteristic of periods in which innovations performed their compensating function effectively. On balance, the bulk of the rise in the L share took place in the first period of the table.

The period 1948–1973 as a whole, during which the "labor share" as here defined rose from about 62 to 70 percent, shows a slightly lower average annual rise of Q/L than of K/L—2.9 as against 3.3 percent. There seems thus to have been a small decline in Q per unit of K. These data are not reliable enough for fine appraisals, but they certainly point to no increase in the Q/K ratio such as would have been needed to hold income from reproducible physical capital—"profits" in that sense (P)—constant in relation to the growing capital stock, when nonlabor income (mainly "profit" income) was declining in relation to aggregate Q. In such circumstances, constancy of the P/K ratio would have required a rising Q/K ratio, which did not occur. Admittedly, only if P were strictly identical with all nonlabor income would this last statement concerning P/K be *algebraically* cogent,[2] but it is clearly a convincing statement in spite of the presence of some other components in nonlabor income.

4. The Problem of Incompatible Income Claims

Returning to Figure 4, we may suggest the following conclusions on feasible long-run growth paths for which demand management policy can successfully aim. Such an equilibrium path cannot establish itself to the right of a "critical point" from the origin. Given correct expectations, the reservation price (supply price) of labor along a growth path located to the right of the critical point would exceed the real-wage rate that employers would be willing to pay. Hence, real-income claims would be

---

[2] It is an algebraically cogent conclusion that, with P/Q declining, Q/K would have to rise to keep P/K unchanged. However, what we have shown is that nonlabor income has been declining per unit of Q, and nonlabor income includes income from nonreproducible wealth in addition to P.

incompatible and the path must be regarded as nonfeasible. A path so described could be maintained only for periods during which inflation of unexpected severity led the public to over-estimate the real incomes they would earn. While such an inflationary process was kept accelerating, and while it thus remained a process of unexpected steepness during successive phases, the labor force would accept money wages whose real equivalent turned out to be disappointing. It is true that employers would turn out to have paid lower real wages than they had anticipated, but this would be of little help to them—partly because productivity trends would weaken and uncertainty increase significantly, and partly because the resulting accounting profits would contain a large nominal component needed for meeting the growing nominal expenses of the next period.

The real reservation price of labor tends to rise as we move the equilibrium growth path to the right on the abscissa because the tighter the labor market the easier the workers find it to get a new job. At the same time, workers know that in a tighter labor market the chances are better that their present employers will yield to their demands. This is why a "critical point" is reached if we move out far enough to the right on the abscissa.

However, the increase in labor's reservation price need not be monotonic as we move the growth path to the right. As we move in that direction, more members of a typical household are employed, and this factor, viewed in isolation, decreases the chances of finding desirable employment opportunities elsewhere. This is one reason why the rise in labor's supply price need not be monotonic as we move the growth path to the right. There exist other reasons as well. As Okun has stressed [34], in tighter labor markets employers find it more advantageous to develop durable ties with a relatively large proportion of their labor force, and the justified belief of workers that their present employers feel committed to their employment in the future may make them more hesitant to change jobs. If, as we move the growth path to the right in Figure 4, real-wage demands do not rise monotonically in relation to the real wages offered by employers, then it depends on demand management policy at what distance from the origin *within the distance defined by the "critical point"* the growth path tends to be established. In such circumstances Friedman's "natural rate of unemployment" [12], which would be a valid concept in perfectly competitive equilibrium, loses its validity.

Furthermore, other characteristics of the growth path would depend on demand policies even on assumptions on which the employment level—the distance of the growth path from the origin—would not depend on demand management. For example, the characteristics of the price trend to which demand policies condition the markets influence the rate of investment. This becomes obvious if we visualize a price downtrend steep enough to raise the real rate of interest since the real rate of interest can clearly not be lower than the rate of price decline.[3] Hence, the tools of demand management policy are powerful in the long as well as in the short run, though they are powerless to move the growth path to the right of the "critical point." Not to observe this latter constraint leads to inflationary disequilibria followed by painful adjustment periods.

A reasonable demand policy should clearly aim for the "critical point"—that is, for the highest activity level establishing itself when price level expectations have become so conditioned that they can be validated by setting aggregate demand at the proper level. At this point, the real reservation price of labor is still compatible with the other real-income claims of the active population.

---

[3] This is so because the money rate cannot fall below zero.

V

Outline of a
Macroeconomic Equilibrium System
and the Problem of Shortcuts

1. The Nature of a Macro-Equilibrium System

In this chapter a simple formalization of a system of macro-equilibria will be developed by recognizing the following:

(a) The usefulness of such a frame of reference depends on the degree to which it gives an acceptable general idea of the conditions that must be satisfied for an economy to move along a normal growth path. Any claim made for an analytical system describing these conditions implies that relatively successful diagnoses and predictions—pragmatic exercises—in an environment of economic fluctuations have *all along been based on the same types of structural relations that are included in the proposed equilibrium system,* except that in those pragmatic dynamic exercises lags are incorporated into the relations and the variables are not postulated to have assumed their equilibrium values. Further, in those exercises the variables and the relationships among them are decomposed (disaggregated) to a significant extent. As was already said, and as will be demonstrated later, such diagnoses and predictions relating to disturbed paths have proved useful, even though they are based in part on formalized dynamic systems that have never been claimed to express adequate general theories and that need to be combined with looser "judgmental" approaches.

Since the system to be developed here is an equilibrium system, the change in the demand for output that occurs when the demand-determining variables change may be interpreted as expressing the changes in demand called for when the equilibrium supply changes. The system then is represented as "remaining" in equilibrium, with deliberate disregard for the route through which it moves in establishing a new state of equilibrium. Alternatively, if the demand-determining variables change without any change in the equilibrium supply, then excess demand or excess supply develops. This will show in the fact that the price level as well as the stocks differ from their expected values—though in what proportions these two phenomena will register the disequilibrium is not formalized here, nor is the route back to equilibrium. Even in the latter case, involving the impact effect of disequilibrating forces, the changes in demand associated with changes in variables will show in the real world with lags because it takes time for the public to develop its reactions, *but a system of this sort disregards even these lags.* Whenever we refer back to our formal system in the analysis of real-world processes, the need to make allowances for lags must be kept in mind. We must remember also that successful attempts to trace disturbed paths of the economy from period to period have so far always merged methods of approach in a way that cannot claim general validity. This will be illustrated in the subsequent chapters.

(b) The framework to be formulated relates to the equilibrium conditions along a *single curve* of Figure 4 (see p. 66). Given the relevant point along a single curve, the gradual vertical upward movements from period to period in a state of macro-equilibrium can easily be formalized, but only on far-reaching simplifying assumptions. There exist sets of assumptions on which the output of an upward-moving system would continue to grow at an unchanging geometric rate, with the real-wage rate likewise rising with a constant logarithmic slope, and the rate of return on capital remaining unchanged. Such assumptions can be fitted into analytical systems making use of aggregative production functions of the Cobb-Douglas or CES variety. It is also possible to construct other assumptions that lead to the result summarized by constancy of the growth rate of output, constancy of the increase in the real-wage rate, and constancy of the rate of return on investment at an unchanging distribution of income. But if we develop such models, we must take account of significant deviations from the assumptions in the real world. The discussion in Chapter IV gives an idea of the direction of some of these deviations (as, for example, rising L share, probably also a declining ratio of P to K).

We now turn to the equilibrium conditions on a single curve along Figure 4.

2. The "Unnumbered Equation" for the Supply of Output (Q)

Given the correctly foreseen general price level $\bar{p}$ to which market expectations have become conditioned, we define $W_1(Q)$ as the wage rate offered by employers for outputs of the various sizes denoted by Q, and we define $W_2(Q)$ as the wage rate for which workers are available for producing these outputs. We now first solve the "unnumbered" equation:

$$W_1(Q) = W_2(Q),$$

to find the supply of Q compatible in our period with the general price level $\bar{p}$, given the fact that wages must be mutually acceptable to employers and workers. If the solution turns out to be a range of Q values, we choose the upper limit of the range and denote it by $\overline{Q}$. If we obtain a single value for Q, this value will be our $\overline{Q}$. For the possibility of a range, see Chapter IV, Section 4. This way of integrating the supply side with the demand side implies "rational expectations" on the part of the public, in the sense that the demand management policies discussed in the next two sections are correctly anticipated by the producers.

3. The Demand Side: The Symbols and Implications

We now face the problem of choosing values for the policy variables in such a way that, given the basic behavioral relations guiding the public, the demand for output will equal the supply described in the preceding section. This should occur at the price level to which market expectations have become conditioned.

Our symbols relate to variables which, given the functional relations to be formulated, will assume values that will not make the decision makers in the markets regret the actions they have taken. When they are making their spending decisions, the income they will earn and the other variables affecting their decisions have in their minds "expected values," presumably with dispersion about these mean values. We here assume that in a state of macro-equilibrium the incomes actually earned and the values of the other relevant variables will make the public feel satisfied with the spending decisions it made, with awareness of the fact that random deviations from the expected values are inevitable. These deviations can usually be reduced by diversification, at some sacrifice in expected values, and this usually seems desirable to the public.

The following symbols will be used:

$M =$ the money stock supplied.[1]

$k =$ the "Cambridge k" (the reciprocal of income velocity).

$p =$ the domestic general price level.

$p_F =$ the foreign general price level.

$p_T =$ the domestic price level of the internationally traded goods.

$Q =$ the period's net output.

$Q_1 =$ the output produced for private domestic consumption.

$Q_2 =$ the output going into net private domestic capital formation, where we may retain some leeway as to which specific durable goods are included in Q_1 and which in Q_2.

$Q_3 =$ the value of goods and services acquired by the government.

$X =$ the net exports of goods and services, that is, the acquisition of foreign claims during the period.

$E =$ the exchange rate.

$T =$ government transfer payments.

$t =$ the effective tax rate on Q.

---

[1] Depending on how inclusive we make the definition of "money," the definition of securities becomes less or more inclusive.

$A =$ the net value of privately held wealth.[2]

$r_B =$ the rate of interest on privately issued domestic securities.

$r_G =$ the rate of interest on domestic government securities.

$r_p =$ the rate of return on domestic physical investment.

$r_F =$ the interest rate abroad.

$b =$ the fraction of the period's private domestic "security issues" which represents additional borrowing from banks during the period.

$N =$ the net acquisition of claims against other countries by official institutions ("support operations" during the period).

If the price level behavior implied in the functions to be formulated should not be constancy of the price level, then expected price changes must be incorporated into several of our functions. This has not been done in our equations. On this problem see Chapter III, Section 7.

As for relations to the rest of the world, we shall imply flexible exchange rates but not exclude support operations by official institutions. The economy under consideration will be assumed to be large enough to have considerable leeway in matters of demand management.

We shall place a bar over all variables that are determined outside the system described in this section—that is, variables that are assumed to be known when this system is being solved. The system will be written as though the fiscal policy variables and the variables expressing official currency-market interventions belonged among these *predetermined* ones, and as though the authorities were looking only for the M which is consistent with the equilibrium requirements. This could be turned around as concerns monetary and fiscal variables; or if we had wanted to formalize a trade-off between these two, then neither of the two should have been assumed given. In that case, however, it would have been necessary to add further equations expressing the

---

[2] This should be the concept of "wealth" guiding the owner in his market decisions. On the difficulties of finding a generally satisfactory definition, see the comments attached to Equations 1 and 6.

assumed trad off, and this would have complicated the present illustration. is essential to include the variables carrying bars, in order to be able to compare different states having different values for these variables.

To simplify matters, r_F will be represented as determined outside the system. In reality, however, foreign interest rates are influenced by those in the country under consideration, but if for this reason we had treated r_F as endogenous, this would have taken us into the problems of foreign economies in general. In view of what was said in Section 2, r_p too is "given" for the single curve of Figure 4 to which the analysis here relates. Also because $p = \bar{p}$, all magnitudes are expressed in current dollars. Observations on partial derivatives will be included after we list the equations.

4. Finding the Values of Policy Variables Ensuring Equality of Aggregate Demand with the Supply Defined in Section 2

In this section ten equations will be presented and explained.

Equation 1:

$$M = k(r_B, r_G, \bar{r}_p, \bar{r}_F, A, \overline{Q}, \overline{T})\overline{Q}.$$

The stock supply of money equals the demand for the stock. The "Cambridge k" (or its reciprocal, the income velocity of money) is a function of the variables appearing in the argument. A bar is placed over Q because that variable has been determined in Section 2. The reason why Q and also T are in the argument is that A does not express the "wealth" of the public adequately *in the relevant sense of the term.* As was explained in Chapter II, Section 5, a steady output or income flow, or even an entitlement to transfer payments, has a "present value" that is not included in private wealth conventionally defined (A). In the argument of k, the variables Q and T are proxies for what Friedman calls human wealth.

Equation 2:

$$\overline{Q} = Q_1 + Q_2 + \overline{Q}_3 + X.$$

84

A definitional identity. As was said in Section 3, we may keep some leeway as to what specific items we want to include in Q_2 and what items in Q_1.

Equation 3:

$$Q_1 = Q_1(\overline{Q} + \overline{T}, \overline{t}, A).$$

The consumption function, expressing the demand for consumer goods. The Multiplier relations mentioned in Chapter I express the fact that as a result of Equation 3 any demand originating as demand for other components of output becomes magnified through the respending of part of the incomes received on consumption.

Equation 4:

$$Q_2 = Q_2(r_B, r_G, \overline{r}_p, \overline{r}_F).$$

This represents a widely used type of investment function, expressing the demand for the goods included in Q_2. In the Keynesian system the marginal efficiency function is of this type.

Equation 5:

$$B(r_B) + S_B(r_B, r_G, \overline{r}_p, \overline{r}_F, A) = D_B(r_B, r_G, \overline{r}_p, \overline{r}_F, A).$$

The stock supply of privately issued domestic securities equals the stock demand. The first term on the left-hand side is the present value of the securities that were outstanding at the beginning of the period. The second term (S_B) is the addition to this supply during the period. The right-hand side is the entire stock demand.

Equation 6:

$$A = A_1(r_B, r_G, \overline{r}_p, \overline{r}_F) + M - bS_B + Q_2 + X.$$

In this simplified form, the value of the stock of privately held wealth consists of the following four components: (1) a function (A_1) of interest rates, expressing the present net value of the non-money wealth that was outstanding in the beginning of the period, (2) the initial as well as the newly acquired money holdings of the public minus the term bS_B, where the last of these terms expresses the addition to the public's debt to the banks associated with the change in M during the period (for

85

S_B see preceding equation), (3) the period's addition to the domestic capital stock, (4) the new acquisition of privately held claims on foreign residents. In this form the equation fails to make allowances for the following facts: part of the current period's change in the government debt affects the net "wealth" of members of the public who do not act in awareness of owing as well as owning that debt; also, the period's private "wealth" in the relevant sense should include additions to the claims of the now active population on future generations even where these claims are not represented by additions to the stock of government securities in any usual sense; and in the event of official currency-market interventions, X is not a precise measure of additions to private claims against foreign nationals. The additions here spelled out verbally amount to a reminder that we have leeway in what to include into the initially outstanding wealth (A_1), and that we should proceed consistently with that decision for the current period's additions (which cannot be enumerated exhaustively in a simplified framework).

Equation 7:

$$G(r_G) + (\overline{Q}_3 + \overline{T} - \overline{tQ}) = D_G(r_B, r_G, \bar{r}_p, \bar{r}_F, A).$$

The first term on the left-hand side is the present value of the stock of government securities outstanding in the beginning of the period. This plus the current deficit equals the stock supply of these securities (left-hand side), which equals the demand for that stock.

Equation 8:

$$E = E(p_T, \bar{p}_F, r_B, r_G, \bar{r}_p, \bar{r}_F, \overline{N}).$$

The spot exchange rate depends on the prices of the internationally traded domestic goods, on foreign prices, on interest rates, and on currency purchases and sales of official institutions. Implicit in the system is the requirement that the forward exchange rate should be consistent with E on the one hand and the differentials between domestic and foreign interest rates on the other.

Equation 9:

$$p_T = f(\bar{p}, \bar{p}_F, E).$$

A change in the exchange rate changes the prices of internationally traded domestic goods relative to the domestic and foreign general price level.

Equation 10:

$$X = X(E, \overline{Q}).$$

Net exports depend on the exchange rate which in turn is determined by the variables in Equation 8.

We now have nine unknowns: M, r_B, r_G, A, Q_1, Q_2, p_T, E, and X. We have ten equations, of which one is redundant and should be eliminated (the choice depending on analytical convenience and thus on the analytical context), inasmuch as we have postulated the equality of all demands and supplies of goods and securities, as well as demand-supply equality for money. This is a well-known source of redundancy.

As for the signs of some of the essential *partial derivatives* in the "normal" case, these must lead to the following conclusions. An increase in the public's after-tax income raises Q_1, but by a smaller amount than the total income increment. Given the price level expectations, an increase in the supply of M through the acquisition of government securities by the central bank lowers the rates on these securities because the public will hold a smaller quantity of these securities at lower rates of return than at higher rates; this tends to lower the rates also on privately issued securities, and when this happens these latter securities become lower-yielding relative to physical capital and this fact raises the security supply forthcoming from private producers, thus limiting the decline of the rates on the privately issued securities and raising the demand for Q_2 goods; at the same time the value of k is raised by the lowering of interest rates. On the other hand, an increase in the supply of government securities raises the rate of return on these, and this tends to raise the rates of return at which the public is willing to hold privately issued securities; this rise, however, becomes limited by a decreased supply of privately issued securities and is associated with a decreased demand for Q_2 goods and with a lower k at the higher interest rates (hence the budget deficits do crowd out private expenditures, but in the "normal" case they crowd out less than the full equivalent of the deficits).

In the general case described by such a system, the demand for money has non-zero finite elasticity with respect to interest, and the same is true of investment expenditure. Hence Hicks's *IS* curve is downward sloping and his *LM* curve slopes upward [21]. Given the rate of return on physical investment, the downward slope of the *IS* curve implies that in the normal case the public's utility functions (risk-appraisal functions) favor diversification and that therefore a change in the asset mix offered to the public exerts an influence on the rates of return on securities (that is, on the "interest rates").[3]

5. Extreme Simplifications along Quantity-Theoretical Lines

Version (a). If in Equation 1 we place a bar over *all* interest-rate terms in the argument of the *k* function, we are thereby expressing the assumption that *k* (or its reciprocal, the income velocity of money) is constant, except for the gradual trend-like effect of rising material and human wealth and of changing rates of return on physical capital along the growth path. This would describe a situation in which the interest elasticity of expenditures is infinite—presumably because of the infinite interest elasticity of the expenditures on Q_2 in which we may decide to include durable consumer goods—and in this case the result would not imply that *k* has zero interest elasticity. The demand for money could be elastic to interest (though not infinitely elastic to it) but an increase in *M* *would not test this elasticity*

---

[3] Hicks's *IS* curve is the *locus* of combinations of the interest rate (measured on the ordinate) and of income (measured on the abscissa) along which planned investment equals planned savings with the result that there is no excess demand in the commodity markets; his *LM* curve is the *locus* of combinations of the same variables (interest and income) along which the demand for money equals a given supply of money. Macro-equilibrium occurs at the intersection of these two curves, since for the corresponding interest rate and income the condition is satisfied that the nonconsumed part of income equals investment expenditure at an interest rate that, jointly with the income level, produces equality of the demand for money with its supply.

since the infinite elasticity of investment to interest would "fix" the interest rate. Hicks's *IS* curve would be horizontal, even if his *LM* curve might *not* be vertical. (The infinite elasticity of *IS* would presumably establish itself with a lag because of the time it takes for the public to react to changes in the variables which determine its expenditures).

However, what the result would mean even in this case of an infinitely elastic *IS* curve is that the public can be shifted to an asset composition that includes more physical capital and claims to such capital than before, and includes correspondingly less securities of the type acquired by the monetary authority, without a change in interest rates (rates of return on securities).[4] The same assumption would also imply that when the public is offered more government securities for its money assets (deficit financing without money creation), it can be shifted to an asset composition that includes less physical capital than before and includes correspondingly more government securities, also without a change in rates of return (or with only transitory changes in the rate structure). Such deficit spending would then crowd out its *full* equivalent in private investment.

Version (b). The assumption that interest rates do not belong in the argument of k (not even with a "bar") would imply that k would not change even if rates of return in the sense of our $\bar{r}_p$ should change—as they would in the event that productivity trends changed—and this *would* in turn imply zero interest elasticity of k. In this case the Hicksian *LM* curve would be vertical. The *IS* curve could be shifting, and the interest rate could be changing, with no change in the demand for money.

To my knowledge few would claim basic validity for either version of the extreme simplification here described. The simplification toward which monetarist writings may be said to "lean to some extent" is our version (a), not version (b). We shall soon see what this means. Yet it is a fact of some interest that a simple heuristic regularity, which in the United States

---

[4] It follows from Tobin's analysis [48] that this amounts to attributing no significance to differences between the risks attaching to different types of assets (see Chapter VI, Section 1).

has been observable for a period of a good many years, gives the *appearance* of a "naive" quantity-theoretical regularity reflecting version (b). As will be explained later, I believe it much more convincing to interpret that regularity in the broader framework sketched in this chapter than by an extreme simplification reflecting version (b) or even by "leaning" in that direction.

6. Extreme Simplification along "Stagnationist" Lines

In Chapter II, Section 4, we saw that in the *General Theory* Keynes was speculating about a future situation in which the elasticity of the k function (and thus of the money demand) with respect to interest rates would become infinite—or at least would become infinite with respect to the rates on the types of security the central banks acquire when engaging in security purchases. This implies a horizontal Hicksian *LM* curve, with the interest rate at a floor level, combined with a downward-sloping *IS* curve. If that situation is envisaged in the long-run context of macro-equilibria, rather than in that of a deep depression creating temporary complications, the picture becomes that of an economy in which investment opportunities have become exceedingly weak or nonexistent.

In such a situation, to make the public shift its asset composition to more money and correspondingly less securities would involve no change in rates of return and no shift to more physical capital. The only way to create more demand would be to raise the Q or the T term in Equation 1 by direct government expenditures and thus also obtain an additional Multiplier effect as a result of the relation defined in Equation 3. For analyzing this problem, one should make the fiscal variables endogenous and M exogenous, because the problem of the policy makers would be that of setting the *fiscal* variables at the level required for equating the demand for Q with the supply determined in Section 2. The money supply would not matter because any additional M would be kept idle (unspent).

Stagnationist predictions did have some credence, especially because for a while the American followers of Keynes had made more of these predictions than Keynes seems to have made. But at present one senses no inclination among neo-Keynesians to attribute much significance to this special case of a "liquidity trap" or "absolute liquidity preference"—particularly not in long-run theory. About impasses that may develop temporarily when, after monetary mismanagement, an economy enters a deep depression no one would like to generalize.

7. Leanings Contrasted with Extreme Simplifications

Practically no economist suggests the validity of either of the theories representing our two extreme simplifications, and since these simplifications do in a sense represent "monetarist" and "Keynesian" extremes, the question is left open what the essential difference is between the neo-Keynesian and monetarists (or quantity theorists) who have become engaged in a controversy attracting considerable attention. The question here is what it means to "lean somewhat" in the direction of one or the other extreme simplification. When infinite or zero elasticities are involved in simplifications and no one wants to commit himself to precise numbers, the question posed by a difference in "leanings" is not a very well defined one.

In the next chapter we shall see that it is nevertheless possible to make sense of a difference in leanings. But I find it confusing that the controversies have been focused so much on this difference between neo-Keynesians and monetarists. At another level of discourse there tends to be a much more essential difference between the economists regarding themselves as "neo-Keynesians" and those considering themselves "monetarists."

VI
Monetarist and Neo-Keynesian Leanings: Useful or Misleading Labels?

1. Simplifications Involving Interest Rate Effects

Our discussion of alternative approaches, including monetarism, will be developed with the problem of demand management in mind, primarily with a view to implications concerning the determination of *money* GNP.[1] The position here taken stresses the need to regulate *nominal* demand, hence money GNP, in such a way as to achieve given price-level targets. This is a different position from one that takes for granted the continued validity under credibly firm policies of those structural relations that have guided pricing behavior in periods when the markets expected to remain unconstrained by any consistently pursued price level objectives of the authorities.

The label "monetarism" suggests emphasis on the role of money. But only on the liquidity-trap simplification of macroeconomic theory discussed in Section 6 of Chapter V is the supply of money irrelevant, and only on the assumptions of the extreme simplification described in Section 5 of that chapter (version [a] *or* version [b]) is the supply of money the only relevant policy variable for the determination of money GNP. We have decided to make differences in this regard a matter of an economist's

---

[1] On appraisals of monetarist contributions to be considered in this chapter see also the papers of Friedman [14, 15], of Brunner and Meltzer [1], of Tobin [50], of Davidson [5], and of Patinkin [36] in Robert J. Gordon, ed., *Milton Friedman's Monetary Framework.*

"leaning" in one of two directions, but if no more than this were said, the suggestion would become very hazy indeed. In reality, there are problems of substantial interest behind this question, and it is possible to make the concept of these "leanings" reasonably articulate. This is well worth doing, even though I consider other differences between the two groups of economists more important.

So far as the emphasis on money is concerned, the pragmatic distinction here is between suggesting that monetary policy should concern itself primarily with regulating the quantity of the money supplied—the money aggregates—by setting M targets that take no account of interest rate effects of the policy, and suggesting that monetary policy should be directed at interest rate effects of the money supply and *through these* at effects on economic activity. Monetarists typically take the first of these two views, neo-Keynesians the second.

The monetarist orientation to money aggregates in this sense implies that large effects of changes in M on money rates of interest frequently reflect no more than the inflationary expectations generated by a steep increase of M or the dampening of these expectations by a small increase of M. If this is the case, monetary expansion *raises* money rates of interest, and the effect of monetary expansion on money rates thus goes in the "wrong direction" by the criteria developed in the main part of Chapter V (where price level behavior and expectations could not be affected). However, it is often recognized by monetarists that, even when the effect of stepped-up money growth on money rates goes in the wrong direction, there may be an effect on real rates that does go in the downward direction assumed in the "unsimplified" general system of Chapter V. From this it would follow that *apart from* the possibility of an induced change of inflationary expectations, stepping up the growth of M by acquiring securities from the public may indeed reduce money rates of interest, at least temporarily and conceivably also in the long run. In other words, monetarists do not necessarily disregard the influence exerted on the structure of rates of return by a change in the public's asset mix—though it was Tobin on the neo-Keynesian side of the controversy who developed the proper theory explaining how that influence is exerted by way of different risks attaching to different types of assets.[2] Nevertheless, when monetarists insist on setting money growth targets directly, rather than setting interest rate targets to be achieved by whatever money growth is required for them, the implication is that we can more easily arrive at general conclusions about the results of specific increases in M than about the interest rate effects of alternative money growth rates and the general economic effects of alternative interest-rate levels. This view *is* characteristic of monetarist writings and this is what I mean by a monetarist "leaning" toward version (a) of the quantity-theoretical extreme simplification described in Section 5 of Chapter V. Nothing is thereby implied about version (b), that is, about perfect or near-perfect interest inelasticity of the demand for money.

According to the monetarist view, it is misleading to judge the effectiveness of monetary expansion by the effect of that expansion on interest rates. Even if we disregard the effects which monetary expansion may have on inflationary expectations, and even if we assume that it has a temporary or lasting interest-rate-*reducing* effect, this effect may be small. It may be small simply because, in the given circumstances, it takes very little change in interest rates to channel large increases in expenditures into the economy. The typical monetarist view so interpreted is, however, not truly representative of the *extreme* quantity-theoretical simplification "version (a)." It would be representative of that extreme only if it were maintained that *apart from effects on inflationary expectations and apart from a brief transition period during which the public has not yet made its additional spending decisions*, an increase in the money supply could not change the money rate of interest *at all* because the money that the central bank creates through its security acquisitions goes into additional private expenditures at an unchanging value of the Cambridge k. This would mean that

---

[2] The gist of Tobin's theory of alternative asset mixes and of the corresponding structure of rates of return is found in [48], where the analysis is given in terms of the theory of personal probability and of utility. See also footnote 4, Chapter V.

private expenditures are infinitely elastic to the interest rate—the interest-sensitive expenditures in question presumably being investment expenditures in which we should include increases in the stocks of consumer goods held by households. Even in this extreme case the interest elasticity of the demand for money would not have to be zero, as was explained in Chapter V, Section 5. Yet the emphasis on money aggregates rather than on interest rate effects of changing the money supply does not necessarily imply anything as extreme as this even about the interest elasticity of private investment, nor is this extreme position ordinarily taken by economists stressing the importance of the money aggregates. What is suggested is merely that the interest elasticity of private expenditures is large enough to make it safer to be guided by the proposition that "changing money-stock aggregates will find their way into expenditures with unpredictable and possibly very small changes in real interest rates and with not much change in the Cambridge k," rather than by the proposition that "changing money-stock aggregates will have an appreciable effect on private expenditures *only* if monetary expansion reduces interest rates sufficiently and if contraction raises them sufficiently."

The second of these propositions—the interest-oriented proposition—is more characteristic of "neo-Keynesian" thinking. The proposition "leans somewhat" toward the other extreme simplification described in Chapter V, Section 6—the liquidity-trap simplification—in a sense which should now be made specific. Here again the position—in this case the interest-oriented appraisal of monetary policy—is not representative of any extreme simplification. It would be representative of one of the extremes discussed in Chapter V only if it were maintained that a change in M typically has no effect whatever on the interest rate because the demand for money is infinitely elastic with respect to interest. In that case the change in M would be fully reflected in the amount of idle (unspent) money held by the public and thus would affect only the value of the Cambridge k at unchanging interest. Hence, this extreme simplification would also negate any effect of M on the interest rate, as does the previous simplification, but for a different reason: the reason for the negation here would be the infinite interest elasticity of the money demand, not of investment expenditure. But the extreme hypothesis so defined is not held by contemporary neo-Keynesians. What *is* held by most neo-Keynesians is that an increase in M will in part go into additional idle deposits at lower interest rates, and that if under the influence of a rising M the interest rate is reduced only slightly, it is because in those circumstances much of the additional M is going into idle deposits at a rising k rather than into private expenditures with little change in k.

The first of these two "leanings"—the leaning characteristic of "monetarism"—also influences an economist's appraisal of fiscal policy problems. The more elastic private expenditures are with respect to the interest rate—and the less government borrowing can influence interest rates for *this* reason—the more will private spending be crowded out by government borrowing at roughly unchanging interest rates and at roughly unchanged values of the Cambridge k. The result will then be that such borrowing for public expenditures will affect merely (or almost exclusively) the allocation of resources between the private and the public sector and will have no noteworthy effect on aggregate expenditures and on the money GNP for a given supply of money. On the other hand, the more an economist accepts the neo-Keynesian supposition that significant changes in the interest rate are needed for obtaining appreciable effects on investment, the more he will be inclined to conclude that the interest-rate-raising effect of government borrowing crowds out much less private investment than would be the full equivalent of the government expenditure. He will conclude that at the higher interest rates money holdings per unit of money GNP—that is, the Cambridge k—will have declined (which is to say that income velocity of money will have risen). In other words, the monetarist position attributes little effectiveness, while the neo-Keynesian attributes substantial effectiveness, to fiscal policy as a tool of demand management.

I think few, if any, would argue that the same assumptions on these matters are justified in all phases of the business cycle. Nor, in my judgment, should the position be taken that even along a normal growth path one of these sets of assumptions is always superior to the other. However, it should be recognized that under flexible exchange rates the effectiveness of fiscal spending policy as a tool of demand management is almost certainly reduced relative to the effectiveness of monetary policy. As was explained in Chapter II, Section 6, when the government engages in additional borrowing and in deficit spending, the effect of rising interest rates on exchange rate movements is apt to work against the expansionary effects of the fiscal operations for some time (with the analogous statements holding for fiscal restraint).

The essential question is whether, in appraising the prospective relationship between M and the money GNP, demand management policy is apt to go far wrong if it pays little attention to any interest rate effects it might produce, except by recognizing that generating inflationary expectations will raise money rates of interest and that this does promote a transfer of assets into interest-yielding forms. In answer to this question, I suggest that in the past thirteen to fourteen years (and in some other past periods) a policy so oriented would have done reasonably well in the United States, provided that it had been guided by a heuristic relation between money GNP and the money aggregate defined as M_2. It will, however, be argued here that the mutual offsetting of various effects has played a large role in producing this result, and that we therefore do not know how long these conditions will last. It thus remains necessary to keep an eye on a broader framework such as that illustrated in Chapter V, supplemented by the appropriate dynamic considerations that must be based partly on formalized systems and partly on looser ad hoc judgments.

Before I explain these statements, it should be made clear that a demand management policy that has generated inflation and inflationary expectations has in fact raised our money rates of interest significantly. From 1960 to 1965 the M_1 stock (currency and demand deposits) was increased at an annual compound rate of merely 3.1 percent, while the M_2 stock (M_1 plus time deposits in the commercial banks but excluding large-denomination certificates of deposit) rose at a rate of 6.2 percent. During this period of small price-level change, short-term interest rates rose much less than they did subsequently, and many long-term rates did not rise at all. From 1965 to 1974, however, M_1 was increased at the much higher annual compound rate of 5.7 percent and M_2 at as much as 8 percent, and during this period of steeply rising prices interest rates, too, rose very steeply. The problem here is not whether it is reasonable to try to hold money rates of interest down by a degree of monetary expansion that steps up the inflation rate: the monetarist emphasis on the unreasonableness of such an attempt is undoubtedly justified. The problem is rather that in one essential respect a radically simplified quantity-theoretical result comes through too well for a specific period to be believed in as a basic regularity and that the result must therefore be placed in perspective.

As was stressed in our analysis, interest rates could be unresponsive (or little responsive) in the longer run to monetary policy even with the demand for money depending significantly on interest rates, since private expenditures and thus the money GNP could be highly elastic with respect to interest. But if we know that, over an inflationary period lasting for many years, money rates of interest have in fact risen steeply and the nominal rate of return on physical investment has also risen, and if in such a period the relationship between a money aggregate and the GNP has remained unchanged, then this gives the impression that those owning the money aggregate are entirely insensitive to opportunity costs. The relation of the money aggregate defined as M_2 to money GNP does give this impression, and at first sight this seems to point to version (b) of the extreme quantity-theoretical simplification defined in Section 5 of the preceding chapter. But a closer look at the problem suggests that in the background of the simple M_2 relation in question there are various processes that must be examined separately.

2. What Is Behind a Simple Regularity?

From the first half of 1962 through the first half of 1974 the money aggregate defined as M_2 grew to 2.5 times its initial size, and the money GNP grew in this same proportion. We shall measure here the income velocity of M_2 by dividing a six-month period's average money GNP (expressed at a yearly rate) by the preceding six month's average M_2 stock. For our span as a whole this income velocity had the mean value 2.47.[3] The standard deviation of the velocity was 0.0218, slightly less than nine-tenths of one percent of the velocity's mean value. Through 1974 the largest deviations were 1.7 percent of the mean upward and 1.5 percent of the mean downward. During the first half of 1975 the M_2 velocity so expressed declined to 2.39 (a more than 3 percent deviation from the mean), but during the second half of the year, after the cyclical upturn, it had risen to 2.47. When defined as the reciprocal of this velocity, the "Cambridge k" was 0.41.[4]

This implies that, beginning about 1962, the ratio of the half-year to half-year increase in M_2 to the half-year to half-year increase in money GNP—the latter increase lagged by one half-year—has tended to unity. In fact, from 1962 through 1975 the average yearly deviation of this ratio from unity has been 1.1 percentage point (in terms of absolute values).

Column 5 in Table 3 shows that in nine of fourteen years the deviation from unity was no greater than the average of 1.1 percentage point (indeed in five of these years it was much smaller); in five years the deviation was larger than the average, and in two cases more than twice as large. The large positive deviations—excesses of lagged money GNP growth over the "corresponding" growth of M_2—occurred mostly in periods in which a reasonable appraisal of policy attitudes was likely to have led the public to foresee a stepping up of the money growth rates from the then recent past. Indeed, the large positive deviations

---

[3] While the January 1976 revisions of the national income and product statistics were taken into account in all figures presented in this chapter, the late-January revisions of recent monetary statistics were not. Taking them into account would have made a negligible difference. The figure to which this footnote is attached would round to 2.48 instead of 2.47, and the next figure to 2.39 instead of 2.38. By far the biggest difference would show for the last figure in Column 6 (the addendum column) of Table 3, which would round to 4.6 instead of 4.8.

[4] The pre-1962 relation of M_2 to money GNP was less simple (not trendless), but over periods of substantial duration it nevertheless was simple enough also to raise the question "what is behind it?" [16, chapters 12 and 13].

Table 3

RATES OF INCREASE OF MONEY GNP AND OF M_2

(1)	Increase in Money GNP over Preceding Half Year (percent) (2)	Increase in M_2 for Preceding Half Year over Half Year Preceding That (percent) (3)	Excess of Column 2 over Column 3 (4)	Excess with Same Lag But for Year as a Whole (5)	Addendum: Increase in M_2, simultaneous with GNP in Column 2 (percent) (6)
1962, I	4.42	2.64	1.78	} 0.87	3.18
1962, II	2.24	3.17	− 0.93		2.47
1963, I	2.46	2.47	− 0.01	} 0.18	3.50
1963, II	3.66	3.50	0.16		3.26
1964, I	3.62	3.26	0.36	} 0.33	2.68
1964, II	2.66	2.68	− 0.02		3.75
1965, I	4.35	3.75	0.60	} 1.61	3.85
1965, II	4.78	3.85	0.93		4.23
1966, I	5.18	4.23	0.95	} − 0.07	4.34
1966, II	3.33	4.34	− 1.01		2.33
1967, I	2.13	2.33	− 0.20	} − 0.20	3.71
1967, II	3.74	3.71	0.03		5.32
1968, I	4.77	5.32	− 0.55	} 0.16	3.76
1968, II	4.45	3.76	0.69		4.65
1969, I	3.79	4.65	− 0.86	} − 1.66	3.90
1969, II	3.16	3.90	− 0.74		0.70
1970, I	2.14	0.70	1.44	} 2.35	1.61
1970, II	2.48	1.61	0.87		4.93
1971, I	5.09	4.93	0.16	} − 3.07	6.59
1971, II	3.51	6.59	− 3.08		4.74
1972, I	5.56	4.74	0.82	} 1.04	4.95
1972, II	5.12	4.95	0.17		5.26
1973, I	6.33	5.26	1.07	} 1.12	4.69
1973, II	4.69	4.69	0.00		4.18
1974, I	3.35	4.18	− 0.83	} − 1.72	4.58
1974, II	3.76	4.58	− 0.82		3.36
1975, I	1.00	3.36	− 2.36	} 1.12	3.63
1975, II	7.17	3.63	3.54		4.84

Note: The half-yearly increases in M_2 and in money GNP are increases from the mean value of a half year to that of the next half year, and the yearly increases from which Column 5 is derived relate to two successive half years. Mean values having been reached some time during a period, the "excesses" in Columns 4 and 5 developed in successive spans that do not end on June 30 and December 31.

101

occurred mostly in periods in which acceleration could already be "simultaneously" observed in those half years and then did in fact continue. The periods in which negative deviations were large tended to have the contrary characteristics—that is, reasonable appraisal of policy attitudes was likely to have led the public to foresee decline in the rate of money growth for reasons which, too, were connected with policy objectives. As can be seen from Columns 3, 4, and 6 in Table 3, this observation clearly holds for the large deviations of 1965, 1969, 1970, and also for the smaller but still sizable deviations of 1974 and 1975. Most readers will recall the generally sensed policy objectives of demand policy ease or restraint in those years. On the other hand, I find the large negative deviation of the second half of 1971 more difficult to interpret in these terms. In general, it is recommended that the reader not overlook the *laglessly* computed M_2 growth rates added in the last column. While for the period as a whole better relations are obtained for the variables with the half-year lag incorporated into the main part of the table, it is nevertheless true that the public, when relating its future expenditures to its present stocks, expects to approximate reasonable objectives for its future "simultaneous" stock-expenditure relations. The lagged stock-expenditure relations are therefore apt to become disturbed if the rate at which additions are made to the stocks (in this case to the M_2 stock) is about to change significantly. Lagged relations may become modified or even put out of commission by simultaneous events.

An attempt to work into broader postwar trends the simple heuristic relationship between M_2 and money GNP leads to the following suggestions concerning these trends:

Trend A. As can be seen from Table 4, there has occurred a substantial and consistent rise in the *ratio of M_5 to the money GNP*. The M_5 aggregate consists of currency and demand deposits (M_1), *plus* time deposits in the commercial banks other than large-denomination negotiable certificates of deposit (the sum so far obtained being defined as M_2), *plus* deposits in thrift institutions (the sum so far obtained being defined as M_3), *plus* large-denomination negotiable certificates of deposit (CDs).

Table 4

M_5 AND ITS COMPONENTS AS PERCENTAGES OF YEARLY MONEY GNP

Year (1)	M_5 (2)	M_1 (3)	Commercial Bank Time Deposits a (4)	Thrift Institution Deposits (5)	Large CDs (6)	Three-month Treasury Bill Rate (7)
1952	58.6	36.0	11.4	11.1	—	1.8
1962	63.8	26.6	15.2	21.3	0.8	2.8
1965	67.9	24.3	17.7	23.8	2.1	4.0
1973	71.7	20.2	21.8	25.5	4.1	7.0
1974	73.0	19.9	22.4	25.4	5.5	7.9
1975	75.0	19.4	23.3	26.5	5.8	5.8

a Excludes large-denomination CDs.

Note: Computed from money holdings representing arithmetic means of December averages for year in question and of December averages for preceding year. M_2 is defined as the sum of Columns 3 and 4. In November 1975, commercial banks were permitted to hold time deposits up to a specified amount for corporations. The effect of this on the relation of M_1 to M_2 has not yet expressed itself to any appreciable extent in the last entries of the table. Note also that a comparison of December 1975 and December 1974 averages would show a decline (not a slight rise) of large CDs relative to M_5 as a whole.

The rise of M_5 relative to money GNP presumably reflects mainly the higher than unitary income elasticity of M_5—that is, its luxury-good character. However, the rate of increase of the M_5/GNP ratio has been influenced also by the general business outlook that at times seemed to justify keeping more liquid assets and being correspondingly less enterprising, or the contrary (note the figures for 1975). It would be difficult to relate the rise in the M_5/GNP ratio to movements in interest rates.

The data give no clear indications of any slowing of Trend A. Note also that if data on Eurodollar holdings were available in the form required for their inclusion in the table, the rise in the aggregate M so broadened per unit of money GNP would be even more pronounced.

Trend B. As for the components of M_5, there has occurred a reduction of the M_1/GNP ratio and a (more than corresponding) rise in the other components of M_5 per unit of GNP. This trend reflects a tendency to accumulate the "luxury good" M_5 in a less

103

"costly," interest-yielding form. Trend B has, however, been slowing. (See Table 4, Column 3.) There are various reasons that may explain a slowing of this trend even when interest rates rise rapidly. For one thing, until quite recently corporations were not permitted to hold time deposits (other than CDs), and even now the amounts they may hold in this form are very limited. Quite apart from this, under conditions other than those of hyperinflation with a corresponding rise of money rates limited to other assets, the public has no intention of moving toward near-zero M_1 per unit of GNP. Yet, interest rates must, of course, be assumed to play a role in determining the degree of shift out of M_1, since the observed reduction of M_1/GNP coupled with a rise of M_5/GNP is induced by the availability of interest payments on all components of M_5 other than M_1. Movements in interest rates must therefore have influenced the speed of the relative shift into these other components. This shows *inter alia* in whatever degree of success has been achieved by multiple regression analysis relating the demand for M_1 to a set of variables including interest rates [17; and 4, pp. 36–39]. Such regressions had a satisfactory explanatory value over a period of many years, but for the latter part of 1975, when short rates declined and GNP rose, they significantly overpredicted the demand for M_1; this suggests that recently, when declining interest rates pulled in the opposite direction (Table 4, column 7), the trend towards a decrease in M_1 relative to money GNP came through more forcefully than the relations expressed by the usual regressions. The broader effect of all relevant facts jointly has so far been a tendency to hold more M_5 liquidity per unit of money GNP *and* to hold it in a less costly form, with the shift away from M_1/GNP decelerating over the period covered in the tables.

Trend C. For the early part of our period, we observe not only a reduction of M_1/GNP, but also a reduction of the M_2/GNP ratio, coupled with rising M_5/GNP. However, the decline in M_2/GNP (Trend C) not only decelerated, but it came to a halt about 1962 and it was not resumed during the period covered in the tables (see the sum of Columns 3 and 4 in Table 4). That is to say, while from 1962 on the additions to "M_5 per unit of money GNP" have continued to be associated with a reduction of "M_1 per unit of money GNP," they have ceased to be associated with a reduction of "M_2 per unit of money GNP." The M_2 aggregate comes closest to M_1 both in the sense that time deposits other than CDs in the commercial banks yield less interest than other components of M_5 and in the sense that the transformation of time deposits in the commercial banks into M_1 can be achieved very promptly at very little cost and effort. Indeed, this transformation has become increasingly easy institutionally with the passage of time. A depositor moves the least far away from M_1 when he remains within the boundaries of M_2. As a result, the slowing of the shift away from the M_1/GNP ratio and the stopping of the shift away from M_2/GNP mirror jointly observable phenomena of a very similar kind. These phenomena may be described by saying that while the increase in M_5 per unit of money GNP so far has not decelerated, the tendency to allow the most "costly" but most liquid components of M_5 to be reduced per unit of GNP *has* decelerated over the period under consideration. In our economy, with a rising standard of living, the trend toward a rise in M_5 per unit of money GNP has been associated all along with a trend toward a smaller proportionate representation of M_2 *in the M_5 aggregate* (see Table 5), and thus with a concern for reducing the opportunity cost involved in holding M_5, but this latter trend has not gone so far as to result in a reduction of M_2 *per unit of money GNP* below the level to which that ratio had declined by 1962. The influence of interest rate movements on this particular result has proved hard to unravel, and this is the particular result that shows in the tendency of M_2 velocity to remain unchanged from 1962 to the end of the period.

To this discussion of main trends in the money aggregates from the early 1950s to the present it needs to be added that over a number of years we have now also observed a tendency that is clearly interest-related, this being the tendency to accumulate the increase in M_5 per unit of GNP in the form of CDs rather than in the form of thrift-institution deposits when interest rates are rising. At the same time, initially small Eurodollar holdings

Table 5
COMPONENTS OF M_5 AS PERCENTAGES OF TOTAL M_5

Year (1)	M_1 (2)	Commercial Bank Time Deposits [a] (3)	Thrift Institution Deposits (4)	Large CDs (5)
1952	61.5	19.5	19.0	—
1962	41.6	23.9	33.3	1.2
1965	35.8	26.0	35.0	3.1
1973	28.2	30.5	35.6	5.8
1974	27.0	30.6	34.8	7.5
1975	25.8	31.1	35.3	7.7

[a] Excludes large-denomination CDs.
Note: See note to Table 4.

were rising at a significant rate. This took place during a period in which much higher interest could be earned on CDs (and, of course, on Eurodollars) than on deposits in banks and in thrift institutions. Thrift institutions have been subject to legal interest rate ceilings only slightly higher than those applying to time deposits in commercial banks, whereas from the large-denomination certificates of deposit—those appearing in the CD columns of Tables 4 and 5—ceilings had been completely removed by the beginning of the 1970s. (For another change in regulations see the notes to Tables 4 and 5.)

Thus, legal regulations and institutional developments in the credit market, including the evolution of new market instruments, have had an influence on some of the trends shown in our tables, and they will continue to have an influence in the future. This introduces a lack of predictability for future trends into the data here analyzed. The other obstacle in the way of trend projection results from the fact that, even with unchanging regulations and unchanging varieties of market instruments, it would be unclear how durable and how independent of interest rate movements in general (and thus of security holdings other than CDs) the post-1962 stabilization of the M_2/GNP ratio would prove to be when accompanied by a continued increase of other

M_5 components per unit of money GNP. It is possible to "make sense" of the recent trends including the tendency of M_2 velocity not to change—because it is reasonable to regard M_5 as a luxury good whose income elasticity exceeds unity and because it would be astonishing if within a framework described by a rising M_5/GNP ratio the decline of the M_2/GNP ratio (and even that of the M_1/GNP ratio) did *not* come to a halt at some point. But there exists considerable uncertainty about the *when* and the *how*. Instead of placing much confidence in the continuation of simple regularities that have in fact been embedded in trends of considerable complexity, we should keep an eye on more comprehensive analytical systems and decide from time to time what the most promising simplifications of these systems are apt to be for a given period.

Over the recent period of more than thirteen years, when the M_2/GNP ratio has tended to constancy and the M_5/GNP ratio has continued to rise significantly, the other conventionally defined "liquid-asset" holdings of private domestic nonbank residents have decreased somewhat in relation to money GNP. These other liquid assets of the owners in question—holdings other than M_5—amounted to approximately 25 percent of their M_5 holdings in 1962 and only to about 15 percent in 1975. However, by their conventional definition these other private liquid holdings do not include Eurodollars.

It should be remembered also that changes in the liquidity position of household and business units cannot be judged merely on the basis of their money or other liquid-asset holdings, because debts have been rising rapidly. Rising indebtedness during the recent inflationary period has been promoted by relatively low money rates of interest that have, in turn, resulted in part from ceilings placed on the rates payable on bank deposits. A rise of money rates smaller than would be the equivalent of expected price increases promotes borrowing, though the fact that money rates are low in comparison with the expected inflation rate of the near future does not necessarily promote long-term borrowing. On the contrary, long-term credit transactions become difficult in circumstances in which the inflation rate is expected to remain high but with considerable uncertainty concerning its magnitude, because the risk-averse lender emphasizes the possibility of particularly steep future inflation, while the contrary is true of the risk-averse borrower. However, during some phases of the recent inflation, short-term rates have clearly been low when measured against the price increases in the following period, and this has created incentives for short-term borrowing. For example, in 1974 the outstanding bank loans of the nonfinancial corporations amounted to 2.9 times as much as in 1965, while the other liabilities of those corporations had grown only to 2.4 times their 1965 level.

3. Appraising the Monetarist Emphasis on M Targets

The dangers of chasing interest rate targets by monetary expansion—especially of obtaining perverse results by generating inflationary expectations—strengthen the case for orienting monetary policy to M aggregates. But this fact does not decide the question whether much attention should be given also to the presumptive interest-rate movements brought about by monetary policy when adjustable M targets are set and appraised jointly with government budgetary targets.

It would be foolhardy to claim general validity for either possible answer to this question. In a framework such as that presented in Chapter V, any answer would require dependable numerical estimates of various elasticities along a normal growth path. Moreover, in the context of cyclical movements, the answer would require a willingness to rely on econometric models of great complexity and on estimates of coefficients that have often proven disappointing. However, it remains the case that, from 1962 on, a simple relation between M_2 and money GNP has proved as good as one could hope, and that any interest rate effects on this relation would be hard to identify.

The kind of framework that was discussed in Chapter V is neither neo-Keynesian nor monetarist. Both monetarist and neo-Keynesian approaches are distinctive only in their way of simplifying matters, and since the appropriate simplifications— the least risky ones—may not be the same in successive periods, one should retain a healthy degree of opportunism in this regard. In fact, we shall see that government agencies that have been quite eclectic in their methodology and have relied heavily on "judgmental" (rather than model-oriented) appraisals of prospective money GNP have accumulated a reasonably satisfactory record. Recently, the record of these agencies has been better than would have been the record of any forecasting method relying exclusively on the regularities showing in Table 3. What has been wrong with the official appraisal of achievable *real* (rather than nominal or current-dollar) results has been an assumption about money-wage and price behavior, given the money GNP. This is the assumption that, even under a firm demand-management policy, money-wage and price behavior could be forecast from the record of past periods in which the public was aware of the authorities' inclination to exploit successively deteriorating short-run Phillips trade-offs. On this assumption no stabilization effort would ever have succeeded in the past. But we shall see that the same authorities who have made this mistake have often made a good appraisal of the prospective money GNP, and their methods have been much more eclectic than methods based on Table 3 above.

The main reason that, in a critical phase of our development, it would have proven constructive to put a greater emphasis on M aggregates than on interest rate targets is that the practical pitfalls in working out the results of monetary policy through interest rate effects have been much worse than the pitfalls in orienting monetary policy to M targets. The most important pitfall in an interest-oriented monetary policy is that when the policy attempts to reduce money rates of interest by increasing the money supply, it may generate inflation and inflationary expectations, thereby unwittingly raising money rates. Furthermore, the trends in the relation between money aggregates and money GNP—trends discussed in the present chapter—deserve considerable attention, and in the explanation of these trends, movements in interest rates do not deserve primary emphasis.

The caveat needs to be stressed, however, that quantitative targets set in terms of money aggregates must be adjustable. There exists no presumption that the same rate of money growth (or money-growth rates falling within a narrow range) will remain consistent over longer periods with given price level objectives and with the best output and employment levels compatible with these. In view of our institutional arrangements, some would also suggest the further qualification that it is necessary to watch interest rate movements carefully because, as a result of the interest rate ceilings on thrift deposits, a rise of money-market rates significantly beyond the interest rate ceiling levels will cause an outflow of funds from the thrift institutions. These institutions play a large role in financing residential construction. The answer to this is that reliance on interest rate ceilings is a particularly harmful, antiquated device for protecting the thrift institutions that in a recent period of steeply rising short rates became exposed to a squeeze because they have lent long and are dependent on borrowing short for remaining in business.

4. Labels that Misdirect Attention

The term "monetarism" has the right connotations when it is understood as suggesting the usefulness of specific simplifications of a more general framework. The simplifications suggested by monetarists tend to deemphasize interest rate considerations in the appraisal of the consequences of changes in the money supply, apart from stressing the dangers of producing "perverse" effects on money rates of interest through monetary expansion. It has been suggested in the preceding pages that the monetarist shortcuts have proved useful—though, as will be seen in Chapter VII, certainly not to the exclusion of other shortcuts. In general, the question of favored shortcuts within the framework of more complex analytical systems is a matter of considerable importance, but it can hardly be regarded as representing a problem in basic economic theory and it is not a matter calling for single-mindedness. Given that neo-Keynesians likewise have an essential money-demand and money-supply function in their system, it is to a question of favored shortcuts that the label "monetarism" directs attention. Problems of a more fundamental character are by-passed by such labeling.

Monetarist and neo-Keynesian views are sometimes said to differ in the emphasis placed on price adjustments as against adjustments of physical quantities when disequilibrium develops. This view is presumably influenced by the fact that the quantity equations include a price term, whereas the initial Keynesian analysis dealt with price effects outside its formal framework. I suggest that the essential difference should be expressed somewhat differently, though the distinction deserving emphasis does have to do with the problem of price effects.

On the macroeconomic level, the truly essential difference is that most economists writing in the Keynesian tradition have attributed equilibrating functions to a rising general price level, while monetarist thinking has paid much more attention to the destabilizing effects of inflationary policies and to the dangers of trying to cope with their effects by using direct controls for suppressing the symptoms. This is the essential difference between the inclinations of most economists considering themselves monetarists and those of most economists usually regarded as neo-Keynesians. But this difference is not well expressed by the label "monetarism."

Nor has the debate become focused on this crucial issue nearly as fully as the issue would deserve. Among our difficulties lending themselves to economic analysis, the most crucial have arisen from the relationship between two sets of reactions: the reactions of the markets to the way authorities behave and the reactions of the authorities to the way the markets behave. The matter is further complicated by the fact that each decision maker in the markets expects the authorities to react not to the way he acts alone, but to the way he expects a large number of private decision makers to act. Clear recognition of the nature of this problem would have led to the gradual emergence of better macroeconomic theory and to better policies. Monetarists may be said to have sensed the importance of this problem more than have neo-Keynesians, but they have not articulated it properly, and they have certainly not placed it in the foreground of their controversies with the neo-Keynesians.

VII
Policy Problems, Present and Future

Over a period of considerable length, policies have reflected the weakest and most outdated elements of an analytical structure that is in need of reconstruction rather than of slight retouching. It has become impossible to continue along the policy lines of the past ten years. We are moving into a period whose characteristics will be different from those of earlier periods, and the change will call for a reorientation of our analytical apparatus. This is so regardless of which way the Western world is going to move—a question clouded with uncertainty—and in any event the time is ripe for taking stock.

1. The Immediate Antecedents: Overexpansion and Commodity Shortages

In Chapter III we saw that in the period from 1951 to 1965 the American authorities had succeeded in keeping the general price trend practically horizontal. The employment policy results of that period could have been improved with the somewhat less inadequate forecasting techniques we now have (see Sections 4 and 5 below). But the policy results of those fourteen years were nevertheless far superior to the results obtained in the following ten-year period which has ended as this book is being written.

The first four years of the ten-year period 1965–1975—the years from 1965 to 1969—had, to be sure, very low unemploy-

ment rates, but the economy was in a state of accelerating inflation, and an effort was made to get price behavior under control
at the cost of a minor recession. What at that time was considered
an acceleration of inflation to a level clearly calling for a shift to
a policy of restraint was an acceleration carrying us for a short
while to an approximately 6 percent inflation rate. Those who at
that time believed the concern with such inflation rates was
exaggerated either revised or at least *would have had reason* to
revise their views at a later stage, since the inflation-dampening
effort at the turn of the decade proved too weak, and the inflation
rate subsequently rose to about twice 6 percent.

Even when this happened, some economists who had all
along shown tolerance for inflationary programs remained
highly critical of anti-inflationary demand-policy efforts. Their
criticism was based on the argument that, partly as a result of
demand-supply discrepancies in the markets for farm products,
partly because of the actions of the oil cartel, and partly because
of movements of the dollar rates, it was impossible to prevent
major *specific* price increases which represent *cost* increases
for the *other* products, and which (these economists argued)
a reasonable policy should accommodate. By "accommodating"
they meant creating sufficient aggregate demand to permit the
pass-through of specific price and cost increases into the CPI
and the general GNP deflator *without* exposing the sellers of
other products to the loss of sales volume corresponding to such
price increases. However, given the inevitability of the burdens
placed on the other sectors by these partly natural and partly
man-made material shortages, this is nothing other than a new
version of the argument that the effects of unavoidable changes
in real-income positions can be covered up by the temporary
fooling effect of inflation.

Supply limitations and bounties that are *unforeseen* cannot,
of course, be prevented from temporarily affecting the general
price level, but these factors tend to cancel out in the longer run
unless policy makers build the effect of supply limitations into
the general price level by raising effective demand. By so doing,
policy makers can give in each stage of the ensuing inflationary
process the impression that it is possible to avoid an inevitable

114

burden, though the burden is in fact merely being shifted back and forth among the various sectors. By 1973–1974 the authorities of most countries showed quite a bit of resistance to the view that policy should in this sense "accommodate" shortages.

When inflation started steepening rapidly in 1973, the authorities moved toward restraint. In the period that followed, they placed considerable emphasis on the need to reduce the rate of price increase substantially. In the United States, from early 1973 on, the rapid rate of monetary expansion was gradually but substantially diminished. Also, in 1973 and in early 1974, the budget deficits declined significantly, in large part because of the disproportionate tax-revenue-raising effect of inflation, given a graduated and unindexed individual tax structure and given a corporate tax structure that includes in the tax base large amounts of merely nominal (inflationary) revaluation gains. However, the sharp economic contraction (particularly in late 1974 and early 1975) raised the budget deficit again. Also, in spring 1975, with the unemployment rate at about 8.5 percent, tax reductions were put into effect to promote economic recovery. The 1976 deficit will be very large by past standards, but monetary policy is now trying to set the growth rates of the money aggregates in such a way as to accommodate only that degree of "real" expansion that is compatible with a gradual decline of the rate of inflation.

In the cyclical peak quarter at the end of 1973 the United States consumer price index had risen at an annual rate somewhat in excess of 9 percent over the preceding quarter, but during the recession—in the fall of 1974—the analogously computed rate of price increase had steepened to a rate beyond 12 percent. Inflation so measured was significantly reduced but was still running about 6 percent when business activity reached its cyclical low and when it was turning up in the second quarter of 1975.

To return to normalcy after an inflationary interlude through which all Western countries went in recent years poses, of course, a more difficult problem than to keep an economy in a reasonably steady state. As was explained in Chapter III, the need to condition market expectations to a reasonably predictable behavior of the price level is not logically identical with a need to establish predictable horizontality of the price trend, but a weighing of the arguments covered in our discussion suggested that a strong case can be made for moving toward that specific target.

2. The Main Difficulty: The Public's Self-Justifying Skepticism about Policy Makers

The difficulties of enforcing a price level target through demand management policy come mainly from the fact that in the given Western institutional setting the public's attitude towards policy makers has become one of self-justifying skepticism. The terminology used outside the economics profession is, of course, different from that used in professional economic analysis, but what the public senses is the great temptation to base policy on short-run Phillips trade-offs, with little regard for the longer-run consequences. It is necessary, in addition, to face some further difficulties, but these are not nearly as weighty as has been suggested by the opponents of demand policy restraint.

In the contemporary Western environment it is the political institutions that place the main obstacles in the way of the authorities whose inclinations might initially be to engage in the consistent conditioning effort needed. The public is sufficiently aware of this fact to develop serious doubts about the credibility of a government asserting its determination to observe price level targets. The skepticism so described could prove to be fatal, because it becomes an element in the kind of circularity which is generally characteristic of games of strategy. There do exist situations in which it is possible to be successful in a strategy described as "I will harm you all if you don't stop harming each other," but once "they" have started harming each other it takes the right moment and the right authorities to be successful in the use of that strategy.

Given full credibility of the policy makers, the effort to condition price level expectations would have an excellent prospect of success without causing major hardship even during the transition phase. With full credibility, cost and price behavior would have to adjust to a demand policy constraint expressing itself in the limited availability of aggregate nominal demand. The less credible the conditioning effort at the outset, however, the more resistance the price trend will show, and the more painful the transition phase will become. The resulting acute discomforts of the transition will then lead to differences of opinion among the policy makers as to the advisability of persisting. These differences of opinion will result in a further reduction of credibility. Assertions of the inherent severity of other obstacles—of obstacles of a more "objective" kind—sometimes rest on misunderstanding, but even to the extent that the further difficulties are real and need to be accepted, emphasis on their severity reflects unwillingness to accept inevitable risks for the sake of avoiding a decisive shift toward comprehensive direct controls. For it must be emphasized that a major economic-political shift in that direction is indeed the alternative to satisfying the price level conditions that must be met if a market economy is to avoid intolerable disturbances.

Account must be taken, of course, of the fact that, when aggregate demand is generated for some specific rate of output growth at an intended price behavior, markets *can* use up this demand in very different ways. This is why so-called stagflation—inflation at low or shrinking output levels—can develop. But account must also be taken of another fact. If the typical decision maker in the markets is thoroughly convinced that price level behavior unacceptable to the authorities causes a recession, it becomes very risky for him to develop individually the type of cost-price behavior that, if generalized, would produce an inflationary pattern. This is why stabilization efforts succeeded in the past, and this is why our price level could be kept stable even during a considerable part of the period after World War II. There is no reason to assume that the basic traits of the population have changed since that time. The public has merely responded to basic changes in policy attitudes, and we all are now hesitant to predict firmly how the attitudes of the policy makers will develop in the future. While a demand management policy lacking determination and credibility is indeed helpless against the public's price resistance, it is the public that is "helpless" against a determined and credible demand-management policy. At the same time it is the public that would benefit from being made aware of this. Such awareness would greatly reduce the public's tendency to generate self-harming processes.

As for the special problems arising even for the most credible and consistent authorities when the point of departure is a significantly disturbed inflationary state of the economy, they develop from the fact that past disturbances (including the inflationary expectations generated by lax policies) have become incorporated in the subsequent cost structure. These difficulties are inevitable, and they raise the question of the relative merits of a gradual policy as compared to one that is sudden and abrupt. A sudden return to a demand management policy aiming for an approximately horizontal price trend has been highly effective after major and violent inflationary inter-ludes but—as a result of initially distorted cost structure—it has often caused significant losses in the market sector. It is prefer-able to avoid losses of that size if, given the size of the preceding disturbances, a gradual approach can still be pursued with suffi-cient consistency. As will be seen later in this chapter, the pres-ent conception of the American authorities is to try to create for the year 1976 an increase in aggregate nominal demand far in excess of the requirements of noninflationary normal growth. This increase is intended to bring about recovery from the reces-sion of 1973–1975 at diminishing inflation rates. This should be the first stage on the road of gradualism, and it *could* lead to a noninflationary normal growth path.

To make an appraisal of the chances for success of such a policy *if consistently pursued* requires forming an opinion of the quality of the foresight of policy makers concerning the aggre-gate demand being generated in successive periods. To this point we shall now turn.

3. Limited but Improving Foresight: Introductory Observations on the "Troika" Forecasts

We shall concern ourselves primarily with the record of the authorities in forecasting *money* GNP in the United States since this is the crucial question for a policy line recognizing that cost and price behavior in the markets can be made to adjust to a generally recognized aggregate-demand constraint. Only a few brief observations will be made at the end of our discussion on the forecasting record for *real* GNP.

From a general theoretical point of view the question is unwieldy because we do not have an acceptable formalized theory of short-run movements of the economy. Indeed, even our formal theorizing about long-run movements along a normal growth path is more illustrative than specific on the role of monetary and fiscal policy and on the role of a number of other variables in the determination of aggregate demand. We do have a good many econometric models that in a sense "answer" questions about specific dynamic developments quite specifically and in considerable detail, but no reasonable person has used these models without significantly adjusting the results. It will be particularly important to make adjustments in working out a policy that attempts to create in the markets a price-expectational mechanism whose characteristics differ from those that determined money-wage and price trends in past periods of lax demand management.

Although there is a sense in which the nature of part formalized and part judgmental procedures cannot be explained or properly understood, their meaning can be sensed by observing any of the "workshops" in which such operations are carried out. By now a considerable number of economists have had an exposure to the way the President's Council of Economic Advisers (CEA) performs this task jointly with the U.S. Treasury Department and the Office of Management and Budget (OMB). On the whole, the procedure has proved reasonably successful in estimating money GNP well ahead of time. This has been the case despite the fact that when programs of the President require legislative action the agencies in question must take the enactment of these programs for granted—even when their enactment is questionable. On various occasions even *real* GNP was forecast with a high degree of precision, but that concerns us less, since the relation between money GNP and real GNP would change with a consistent conditioning of price level expectations to policy targets. The trend has been toward improvement of the forecasting record.

The CEA-Treasury-OMB estimating or forecasting team has been nicknamed the "Troika." Its procedures have been heavily "judgmental," one reason for this being that consensus must be reached within the team. The econometric models of prominent private forecasters as well as intramural (governmental) econometric models have indeed been regularly consulted in these procedures. But the estimates have been based in large part on recent information of a more ad hoc character and on past or expected relations among the data to which such pieces of information relate. It has, of course, been recognized that details of the estimated course of the economy must make up a consistent whole. Since 1962 the Annual Report of the CEA, which is published either at the end of January or on one of the first days of February each year, has presented for each successive year an overall estimate of money GNP and of its real counterpart, and also estimates of some of the components of these aggregates. The same January forecasts are used in the President's budget message and in the documents supplementing it. These documents are likewise published at about the same time.

As the year progresses, revisions are made and occasionally these revisions receive publicity, but in this regard there exists quite a bit of institutional inertia. The reason is in part that government agencies must agree on the revisions, and in part that there is a difference between being obliged to make a numerical estimate for the budget and for the CEA report around the turn of the year on inevitably shaky grounds and volunteering to do so subsequently. In any event, what interests us here is the quality of the foresight of policy makers *well ahead of time,* because that is the kind of foresight needed for policy decisions. Policies take effect with a lag, and demand policies of the fiscal variety, in contrast to monetary policies, cannot even be adopted without a considerable lag. We shall therefore consider the record of the past fourteen years for predictions made well ahead of time, and we base our appraisal on the Annual

Report of the CEA for the calendar year at the beginning of which the report was published.[1]

4. The Forecasting Record from 1962 to 1975

During the five years from 1962 through 1966 the CEA's predictions show an average deviation of 1.5 percent from the realized money GNP levels. Four predictions were underestimates, ranging from 0.6 to 2.4 percent, one was an overestimate by 1.5 percent. In none of the following nine years was the error ("deviation") as great as even the second largest in the period from 1962 through 1966.

During the nine years from 1967 through 1975 the average deviation from the realized levels was 0.7 percent. Five predictions were underestimates, ranging from negligible to 1.7 percent, four were overestimates ranging from 0.5 to 1.0 percent.

The following method was used for obtaining these figures. If in the month of January of the year t the CEA report estimated the money GNP of the year t at y dollars, having at that time a preliminary estimate for the money GNP of the year $t-1$ amounting to x dollars, this was interpreted to mean that according to the estimate money GNP would change in the proportion y/x.[2] Assume for illustration that this was a rise of 6 percent year over year. That rise was compared with the "actual" rise of money GNP from $t-1$ to t, as disclosed by hindsight. In the application of hindsight, the so-far-latest GNP statistics were used for those two years, except that in this operation the January 1976 benchmark revisions were left out of account (with an inevitable minor inconsistency developing from the fact that for the "actual" rise from 1974 to 1975 the

---

[1] Before 1962 the CEA reports contained no such forecasts. Okun's 1959 study [33] of the problem of forecasting errors for the years 1955-1957 suggests that the *private forecasts* included in his sample came out on the average *very* poorly by our present standards for 1955 and for 1956, though (particularly for money GNP) very well for 1957.

[2] The y dollar "preliminary" figure for $t-1$ is found in the statistical appendix of the CEA report published in t.

unavailability of pre-1976 statistics on the 1975 GNP made it necessary to use for *that* "actual" rise figures that included the 1976 revisions).[3] Say that with such hindsight the actual increase from $t-1$ to t was 6.5 percent, as compared to the 6 percent estimated increase derived above. The level of the money GNP was then said to have been underestimated in the proportion 1.06 to 1.065—that is, by 0.47 percent. In such a case the rate of change was said to have been underestimated in the proportion 60 to 65, that is, by 7.69 percent. The average deviations were rounded to the first decimal.

The 0.7 percentage point average deviation for the period 1967 through 1975, as expressed in terms of the *level* of money GNP, represents, for obvious reasons, a very much higher proportion of the *rate of change* from one year to the next. During the period 1967 through 1975 the average deviation of the projected *rate of change* of the money GNP from the actual *rate of change* (in all years an increase) was close to 10 percent of the actual. During the period 1962 through 1966, when the average deviation in levels had been 1.5 percent, the average deviation in rates of change had been close to 21 percent.

During the nine years 1967 through 1975, the most radically simplified quantity-theoretical method, based on the M_2 aggregate and postulating a half-year lag as described in Chapter VI, Section 2, would have yielded an average deviation of rates of change amounting to almost twice the deviation of the Troika forecasts, when the deviation of the estimated from the actual rates of change is expressed as a percentage of the actual. However, for the earlier period 1962 through 1966, the method described in Chapter VI would have yielded on the average less than one half the rate-of-change deviation computed for the Troika forecasts. Indeed, when so viewed, the radically simplified quantity-theoretical method would have led to better results through 1968. Yet one reason why the two methods are not comparable for the present purpose is that part of the information

---

[3] For no year before 1975 would the inclusion of the 1976 revisions have made a difference of more than 0.2 percentage points in computing the "actual" rise so defined. However, these benchmark revisions were major, and it seemed preferable to make no allowance for them in the interpretation of hindsight in the sense here relevant.

used in Table 3, Chapter VI, was not available in the months of January, and that quite a bit of guesswork would therefore have been involved in using that method at the time the Troika forecasts were made.

The main conclusion is that whereas at the present stage of knowledge we cannot articulately describe the combination of methods used by forecasters, they have gradually acquired a reasonably good record of predicting money GNP. This, of course, is not quite the same thing as being reasonably dependable in appraising the consequences of demand management policy, or the consequences of any specific set of variables entering into forecasting exercises. A forecasting record may benefit from offsetting errors. Still, there is no contradiction between denying that we have a usable articulate theory of movements along disturbed paths of the economy, and nevertheless asserting that to aim for a level of money GNP falling within a narrow range has become a reasonably promising endeavor.

We have explained why the past forecasting record for real GNP is less relevant for the purpose of the present analysis than the forecasting record for money GNP. The CEA forecasting record is much poorer for real than for money GNP, but not because for real GNP there would have been a significantly greater average deviation of the projected from the actual level during the past five years. In terms of levels, the average deviation for the real GNP *is* somewhat higher than that for money GNP during the years 1967 through 1975, but not very much higher.[4] However, the record for real GNP is much worse in another sense. What needs to be remembered is that, when we compare the forecasting record for real with that for money GNP, *slightly* higher deviations for *levels* of real GNP correspond to *very much larger* errors for year-to-year *changes*. This clearly would be so even if the sign of the change in real GNP had been forecast correctly in each year, because the growth rate of real GNP has been much lower than the rate of increase

---

[4] On several occasions some amount of leeway was left by the CEA for a reasonable quantitative interpretation of the council's real-GNP expectations, but the leeway was never very large. For 1966 through 1975 I obtained a 1.1 percent average deviation from the actual levels, as compared to 0.7 percent for the money GNP.

of money GNP. But the algebraic sign has also caused difficulties. When year-to-year declines occurred, these were not predicted successfully in the months of January, and the only cyclical turning point that was forecast correctly was the upturn that occurred in the spring of 1975.

5. The Break in the Mid-1960s

During the period 1951–1965, in which the price trend may be regarded as "practically horizontal," money GNP increased at an annual compound rate of 5.2 percent. It makes no difference here whether we use the unrevised data for money GNP or take account of the January 1976 benchmark revisions, though some irrelevant details in Table 6 are influenced by the revisions. I did in fact take these into account here.

It can be seen from the table that up to 1963 the year-to-year increase in money GNP never remained above the 5.2 percent average by more than 0.2 to 0.3 percentage points for longer than a single year. The increase was, however, much higher for the single years 1955, 1959 and 1962, and these followed years with significantly subnormal increases. On two occasions significantly subnormal increases lasted for one year, on a third occasion for two consecutive years. There was more instability both in the rate of increase of the money supply and in the rate of change of the GNP than one would hope for under a future policy aiming for reasonable average rates of expansion.

The post-1965 period with its different policy attitudes is foreshadowed in the data relating to the one- to two-year period immediately preceding that year. Since 1963 the rate of increase of money GNP has remained significantly above normal by past standards. Apart from brief interludes, this rate of increase in money GNP was supported by supernormal increases of the money supply, without which this development could not have taken place. By 1964 the unemployment rate had declined to 5.2 percent for the year as a whole, and the year's 5.3 percent real-GNP growth rate contained an appreciable cyclical expansion component. At that time a tax reduction program was put

124

Table 6
YEARLY CHANGES IN GNP AND IN M_2, AND THE BUDGET SURPLUS

| Year | Percentage Increase over Preceding Year of: | | | Federal Budget Surplus of Year (NIPA basis) |
	Money GNP	Real GNP (1972 prices)	M_2	
1952	5.1	3.8	5.4	−3.7
1953	5.5	3.9	3.8	−7.1
1954	0	−1.3	3.5	−6.0
1955	9.0	6.7	3.7	4.4
1956	5.4	2.1	1.7	6.1
1957	5.2	1.8	2.6	−2.3
1958	1.4	−0.2	4.8	−10.3
1959	8.4	6.0	4.7	−1.1
1960	4.0	2.3	1.0	3.0
1961	3.4	2.5	5.2	−3.9
1962	7.7	5.8	5.8	−4.2
1963	5.5	4.0	6.5	0.3
1964	6.9	5.3	6.3	−3.3
1965	8.2	5.9	8.0	0.5
1966	9.4	5.9	7.7	−1.8
1967	5.8	2.7	7.7	−13.2
1968	9.1	4.4	8.9	−5.8
1969	7.7	2.6	6.6	8.5
1970	5.0	−0.3	4.5	−12.1
1971	8.2	3.0	11.7	−22.0
1972	10.1	5.7	10.2	−17.3
1973	11.5	5.3	9.6	−6.9
1974	7.7	−1.8	8.5	−11.7
1975	6.5	−2.0	7.9	−73.4

into effect to strengthen the expansion. In 1965, when money GNP rose by more than 8 percent, and the real growth rate moved up to 5.9 percent, and when unemployment declined to 4.5 percent, the rate of increase of the money supply was stepped up appreciably.

Thereafter, in the four years following the fiscal year 1965, the Vietnam War raised defense expenditures from $48.6 to $80.2 billion (with a small reduction of the current dollar amount in the following four years), and federal nondefense expendi-

125

tures were raised from $69.8 to $104.3 billion (with an even steeper increase of transfer payments subsequently). The methods of financing these expenditures showed great concern with keeping activity levels high and little concern with the fact that inflationary techniques are unsuitable for achieving this objective for more than a very limited period. Shortly after 1965 large budget deficits began to emerge and, apart from two brief spans in 1966 and 1969, the rate of increase in the money supply moved into increasingly high regions until 1973. The cost and price behavior that we now find so difficult to bring back to normalcy began to develop about 1965 *not because the public acquired different characteristics but because the policy makers had started behaving differently.* Now, after many years, some signs of a more-than-temporary change of mind may perhaps be observable in this regard, but these signs are of very recent origin.

The steepening rate of price increase in the post-1965 period was discussed in Chapter III, and data were presented there on the low unemployment rates of the years 1965 to 1969 as well as on the unfavorable unemployment record that followed. From 1965 to 1973 money GNP increased at an average compound rate of 8.0 percent (as against 5.2 percent for 1951–1965), and real GNP grew at an average rate of 3.6 percent (as against 3.4 percent for the earlier period). However, the calendar year 1975 shows a 3.8 percent decline in real GNP from 1973. Hence, for the ten years from 1965 through 1975 the average compound rate of increase of real GNP was only 2.5 percent. The rate of increase of the GNP deflator for that ten-year period was 5.3 percent (with the highest annualized quarter-to-quarter compound rate of 12.5 percent reached in the last quarter of 1974). The unemployment rate for 1975 came out at 8.5 percent, having hit a somewhat higher level around the trough of the recession in spring 1975.

6. Gradualism and Abruptness

When the recession had bottomed out in 1975, the policy variables were set in such a way as to correspond to an expected 12 percent rise of money GNP from 1975 to 1976, year over year, and to a similar (slightly smaller) increase *during* 1976. Such yearly increases of money GNP might turn out to be the largest ones of the post-Korean period, because of the intention to accommodate, for the time being, quite a bit of inflation—even if at an appreciably reduced rate as compared to the preceding two years. Also, along with what is expected to become a significantly reduced inflation rate, the roughly 12 percent increase in money GNP is intended to accommodate cyclical recovery of real output from its recession level at a rate no faster than is believed to be compatible with appreciably diminished inflation. This expresses the essence of the current strategy: whether that strategy will be followed through in the coming years is a matter of guesswork not merely for the economics profession but for the markets as well. Some of the official statements and documents suggest the needed determination, others do not.

The proper strategy requires, of course, a gradual diminution in the rate of increase in money GNP from the initial post-recession rate. If the return of the activity level to normalcy is not to be interrupted by repeated recessionary interludes, the pace must be moderate even during the early stages of the recovery. A subsequent effort to reduce the year-to-year rate of expansion by a large margin when the economy approaches its normal growth path would very probably result in contraction rather than in merely slowing the expansion. The gap between a 12 percent (or conceivably somewhat larger) initial year-to-year increase in money GNP and anything like the 5–5½ percent average increase of the pre-1965 period would be very large—too large to be manageable in one further year and probably even in two further years along an uninterrupted cyclical recovery path. In the entire post-Korean era (as can be seen from Table 6) the largest year-to-year reduction of the rate of increase of money GNP *not* associated with a recession was the reduction from 9.0 to 5.4 percent from 1955 to 1956—a 3.6 percentage point reduction. From 1966 to 1967 we had a reduction of the increase of money GNP by the same margin—from 9.4 to 5.8 percent, and this was associated with what some analysts describe as a mini-recession.[5] Abruptness has its obvious costs. On the other hand, the risks of gradualism are those of a loss of patience, particularly in an environment in which political groups are often trying to outbid each other with promises relating to the immediate future.

7. Subsistence Guarantees, Market Power, and the Problem of Measured Unemployment

De facto subsistence guarantees by way of transfer payments were spreading in the Western world even before our economies were exposed to the aftermath of accelerating inflationary processes. Arrangements of this sort would have to be worked into any program for a slow return to activity levels thereafter to be considered normal. This is another reason for recognizing the existence of a problem of strategy for governments in their relations with the public, because quasi-guarantees of this sort become worthless if the proportion of the population desiring to place itself on the receiving side grows too large. I have no numerical estimate how large is too large, but it is obvious that the difficulties which Western countries need to face in meeting this problem may become substantial.

In 1975, government transfer payments to individuals amounted to 14 percent of all personal income in the United States, this being a proportion that has risen steeply over the past quarter-century. It must, of course, be remembered that 1975 was a year with an exceptionally high unemployment rate, and it must be added also that social security benefits account for

---

[5] As for the recessions in the true sense, that of 1957-1958 was associated with a 3.8 percentage point reduction of money GNP growth from the first to the second of these years, followed by a subsequent rapid increase; the 1960-1961 recession shows in the yearly data in a 4.4 percentage point reduction of money GNP growth from 1959 to 1960 and another 0.6 percentage point further reduction of the increase from 1960 to 1961; the 1969-1970 recession was associated with a 1.4 percentage point reduction of the increase of money GNP from 1968 to 1969 and a further 2.7 percentage point decrease from 1969 to 1970; and the 1973-1975 recession was associated with a 3.8 percentage point reduction of money GNP growth from 1973 to 1974 and a further 1.2 decline of that increase from 1974 to 1975. Due to timing within the years, the *yearly* real GNP data in Table 6 understate the sharpness of the 1957-1958 recession as compared to the others prior to 1973.

about 47 percent of all government transfer payments and government retirement benefits for another 13 percent. But as the social security system is organized in the United States, it would be misleading to put it into a different category, because the benefits do not represent the yield of capital saved earlier by the beneficiaries. Instead, they involve transfers from those employed in any period to those already retired. Nor will those "now" contributing receive their future benefits in proportion to their contributions, quite apart from the fact that appreciable future increases in tax contributions will be needed to meet future costs. Costs have been rising rapidly, in part because the benefits have been indexed and in part because they have been raised significantly in real terms. Nevertheless, there does exist an essential difference between social security and most transfer payments. In general, the network of transfer payments that has developed in the Western industrialized world provides one of the main reasons why it is impossible to draw a clear distinction between involuntary and voluntary unemployment, yet social security has this particular consequence to a lesser extent than transfers that are available regardless of age and health.

Networks of transfer payment entitlements are likely to be more systematically developed in the future than they are now, and only if a number of conditions are satisfied will any such system prove manageable. One of the main economic conditions to be satisfied is that limitations on competition by groups possessing market power should not reduce favorable work opportunities too greatly. Other equally important economic conditions are that the terms of subsistence guarantees should not become too tempting, and that the required tax revenue should not be collected with reliance on a tax *structure* whose characteristics seriously damage incentives. Quite apart from strictly economic conditions, there is, however, the very important general sociological requirement that a sufficiently large proportion of the population should derive satisfaction from performing a useful function in the economy rather than live on transfers. Analogous conditions apply to arrangements involving ad hoc activities of the work-relief type in the public sector or in the nonprofit sector in general. The partly economic and partly general sociological conditions for the manageability of a system involving essentially "guaranteed" subsistence are complex enough to prevent any reasonable person from making unconditional assertions about the future of these systems. This difficulty may, however, be expected to grow less weighty with the progress towards normal activity levels during the recovery, unless political trends favoring the relative growth of the transfer-supported population should prove so strong as to offset the effects of recovery.

There are uncertainties about quasi-guaranteed subsistence, but there is no uncertainty about the fact that the policy of trying to "guarantee" full employment has proved a failure. By "guaranteed" full employment in this sense I mean the achievement of numerically specified low ranges of measured unemployment. The only systems that can live up to such a guarantee are those in which being on a payroll is in many cases hard to distinguish from receiving transfer payments without performing any useful function, or in which the judgment asserting the usefulness of a function performed is political rather than derived from the observed behavior of the public.

The existence of market power in many areas is an inevitable property of modern market economies, even of economies that on the whole are keenly competitive. The market power of groups of producers and of groups of workers inevitably leads to some exclusion of would-be rivals, with the result that equally remunerative opportunities are not open to those rivals. While this adverse influence could and should be reduced by policy measures such as trade liberalization, deregulation, and antitrust, relative real-income positions will always reflect market power to some extent. In the United States there is no clear evidence so far of an increase of complications arising from this factor; in some other countries significantly increased difficulties arising from this source have clearly complicated the task of keeping employment levels high. But it is generally true that in circumstances in which cost and price trends are influenced by market power as well as by minimum-wage provisions, *and* in which at the same time the burden of being temporarily unemployed is significantly reduced by "transfers"—cash payments and benefits in kind—the government cannot truthfully promise to keep the measured unemployment rate in a specified low range. A government that makes such a promise and attempts to live up to it by generating inflation of unexpected severity will have to face the consequences. Workers will discover after a while that their real wages are lower than those they expected to earn when they entered into their obligations, and investors will discover that their real rates of return do not justify the commitments they have accepted.

8. Turning from the Spurious Distinction between Voluntary and Involuntary Unemployment to Substantive Problems

On the negative side, the basic fact of which policy makers must become conscious is that in the contemporary environment neither the Keynesian nor any other general distinction between involuntary and voluntary unemployment can serve as a guide to policy. It would be difficult to raise a more unwieldy and useless question than whether a person counted as unemployed in our surveys is unemployed because he or she has knowingly insisted on wage demands likely to keep him or her unemployed, or because the person has miscalculated the effect of the wage demand made, or because institutional arrangements have prevented a reduction of a wage demand.

The principle that *can* serve as a useful guide to policy is that demand management should accommodate the highest activity levels that develop when the behavior of the price level is not significantly misjudged by the public—that is, when price level expectations have become adjusted to credible targets of the policy makers. It is essential to remember that the activity levels so described depend on which institutional rigidities we regard as desirable or at least acceptable, and which we are willing and able to reduce or to eliminate [20, 47].

To suppress collective bargaining or to eliminate all institutional support for the needy would greatly reduce rigidities, but by a method practically no one would favor. Either of these changes would enable demand management to move to a lower

131

level of unemployment without violating consistently pursued price-level objectives. Yet *even* if these were acceptable changes we would not justifiably conclude that a successful demand-management policy could reduce unemployment to a "voluntary" component. Major employers would still be faced with a collective of workers, and in their hiring and firing practices they would have to be mindful of problems of morale. They could not afford to fire a major proportion of their workers whenever others offered their services for a lower wage. Workers on the job would know this and would behave accordingly.

Essential social-political objectives of late twentieth-century communities would, of course, be violated by abolishing institutional support for those incapable of supporting themselves or by trying to force large bodies of workers to represent their joint interests in a clandestine fashion with a threat of penalty. But it would be wrong to conclude that the whole system of wage- and price-rigidifying regulations, developed in good part under the influence of specific interest groups of employers and workers, reflects the consciously maintained value judgments of the community and should therefore be considered immutable. It is exceedingly likely, for example, that a high proportion of those who favor the protection of low-income recipients thoroughly misjudge the consequences of minimum-wage legislation on the unemployment rate, and that a large number of measures protecting specific groups of workers and of producers by legally sanctioned barriers has effects that are also widely misjudged by the public. Nor is the crucial significance of free trade as a means of antitrust in the broader sense properly understood. What a reasonable demand-management policy can achieve depends to an important extent on attitudes to rigidifying factors: these rigidifying factors are of different types and should not be judged jointly.

The implications of striving for the minimum measured unemployment rate consistent with a price level behavior to which market expectations have become conditioned also depend to an important extent on our methods of measurement. By the present methods of measurement in the United States, and given our present institutional arrangements, a gradual and substantial diminuation of the close to 8 percent early post-recession rate is very likely to occur during the present recovery, but there exist no firm grounds for specific numerical statements about the measured unemployment rate along our future "normal growth path."

Our monthly survey method counts as unemployed all persons aged sixteen or over who, according to someone found at home in the household in which the person lives, has no work but is currently available for work and has been looking for work some time during the past four weeks, *or* will report to a job as of a date no more than thirty days ahead. From this information, however, we cannot conclude anything about the intensity of the effort made to find work, nor about the conditions under which employment would be accepted by the person in question, nor even about job offers that may have been turned down. Those who receive unemployment compensation are required to be available for a job that is suitable to their work experience and does not require moving out of the region in which they live, but in most places this requirement is believed to be administered quite leniently. Recently, the American unemployment compensation system has been extended significantly both in coverage and in duration.

As for the conditions of employment accepted by the labor force, the data suggest that during the recession, when from the peak quarter to the second quarter of 1975 the measured unemployment rate rose from 4.8 to 8.7 percent, average real-wage rates declined by about 3 percent. There is every reason to assume that this happened in a period in which the impending inflation rate was underestimated by a considerable margin and in which therefore the "real" equivalent of the agreed-upon money wages was expected to be higher than turned out to be the case. The decline in real-wage rates has now been reversed. This implies that even a measured unemployment rate which at this writing still is 7.5 percent weakens wage demands no more than is compatible with a renewed *rise* in acceptable real wages. This in turn implies that quite a bit of intellectual acrobatics are needed for labeling such unemployment as involuntary. It would, however, be equally wrong to jump to the conclusion that it is voluntary.

133

Not only does the distinction between voluntary and involuntary unemployment lack "operational" content but, in addition, it is psychologically unrealistic by even the loosest criteria one may be willing to apply.

What we do have reason to accept as a fairly good description of reality is that in the cyclical peak year 1973, some 42.2 percent of the civilian noninstitutional population aged sixteen years or older was not working; of the persons belonging in this category 7.0 percent were regarded as unemployed—so regarded because for them the household surveys provided the information described above. Further, in the cyclical trough year 1975, 44.0 percent of the civilian noninstitutional population was not working; and of the persons belonging in this category 11.8 percent were regarded as unemployed, for the same reason. Since the civilian labor force is defined as consisting of those working (outside the armed forces) plus those who are unemployed by the foregoing definition, the measured unemployment rate was 4.9 percent for the year 1973 on the average, and 8.5 percent for 1975, as expressed in relation to the civilian labor force. But it is impossible to arrive at a sound judgment on the voluntary or involuntary character of the unemployment of 7.0 percent of the nonworking population in 1973 or of 11.8 percent of the nonworking population in 1975. This is so quite aside from the fact that even in 1975 more than 10 percent of those counted as unemployed became jobless by leaving their jobs ("quitting")— a proportion that approximated 17 percent in the late part of 1973.

There are several reasons why distinguishing elements of voluntariness from elements of involuntariness in the unemployment problem is a hopeless endeavor. It must be obvious to any observer that the intensity of the job-seeking effort of those counted as unemployed is apt to vary widely, and that for organized workers the wage demands are made by unions rather than by job-seeking workers individually, and that there exist other categories of workers to whom minimum-wage laws apply. Nor do technically unorganized workers of major establishments behave as bodies made up of atomistic units, certainly not if unionization is an available alternative, and not even if unioni-

134

zation is left out of account. Furthermore, even an individual worker acting "atomistically" would have reason to weigh the advantages of holding out for his wage demands against the risks of being temporarily out of work. This holds true especially in view of the recent appreciable extension (up to sixty-five weeks) of entitlement to unemployment compensation. These are the reasons why real wages may be rising—that is, why such a wage trend is not underbid by job seekers—when 7.5 percent of the civilian labor force is counted as unemployed. Yet, on the other hand, it must be remembered that in a recession the chances of obtaining a desirable job after a short while turn out to be considerably worse than many are likely to have expected initially. During the recession of 1973–1975 the average duration of unemployment rose from less than ten to more than sixteen weeks, and the long-duration ("fifteen weeks or longer") component of the total rose from less than 1 percent of the civilian labor force to about 3 percent.

The willingness of employers to yield to inflationary wage demands and the insistence of workers on these demands depend on the expected behavior of those in charge of demand management policy. This does not mean, however, that the measured unemployment of a transition period *or* of periods of normal growth could be decomposed into a voluntary and an involuntary component. In most cases, even the situation of a single unemployed person cannot be so decomposed. Nor is it generally legitimate to place persons in different categories of presumptive involuntariness or voluntariness depending on whether they are "looking for a job" on unrealistic conditions or are not looking for a job because they know that none is available to them on the conditions on which they would be willing to accept work.

9. The Alternative

For reasons explained in Chapter I, transition to a system of administrative wage and price controls is the alternative to a credible demand-management policy directed to the highest activity levels consistent with reasonable price-level targets. The analysis in Chapter III, Section 7, suggests that "reasonable price-level targets" should in all probability be interpreted as involving a gradual return to a practically horizontal general price trend. In a debate in which we are trying to come to grips with one of the most essential problems of our times there is no justification for talking around the subject by avoiding the term "wage and price controls" and substituting for it such words as "jawboning," "social contract," "social consensus," "incomes policy," and so on. These expressions have begun to proliferate, but either they represent mere political sugar-coating or they describe no more than the spotty and arbitrary use of governmental powers under the influence of political group pressures. They do not describe ways of improving the results that develop from a market system. Nor is there reason for expecting viability of the wage and price *structures* that are inevitably implied in tax-subsidy schemes occasionally proposed for preventing "undesirable" wage-price behavior by means of democratically legislated "carrots and sticks." It is, of course, possible to get lost for a long time in a region of ineffective selective interferences inspired by vote-getting considerations, and it is possible thereby to weaken greatly a country internationally. But even if history could take that turn in some countries, it would be morbid to try to construct a theory of how best to achieve *that* result.

A system of comprehensive direct wage and price controls *is* an alternative to be taken seriously. Given the present political structure of the Western world, transition to direct controls would not be smooth, since the required institutions and the required willingness to obey unconditionally are lacking. Comprehensive controls call for heavy reliance on police power, and the number of would-be violators with whom Western law-enforcement apparatus can cope is very limited. We are not doing particularly well about mugging in the streets, and the impulse to sell one's goods and services on the most favorable terms acceptable to buyers has so far remained much more generally characteristic of our population than the impulse to mug.

Not even a comprehensively controlled political and economic system could, of course, reconcile a full employment program with a program greatly reducing the disadvantages suffered by persons when they are out of work. On the other hand, such a system could directly or indirectly force many more people onto payrolls. Further, it might be able to keep a regulated price level constant, and it could regulate income differentials. What goods would be available at those wages and prices is another question. In particular, it is practically impossible to develop criteria for the appropriate profits "permissible" to investors engaging in risky innovations in circumstances where the unsuccessful are not compensated for their losses. The incentive to innovate would in all probability be greatly reduced in those circumstances.

But there is a sense in which rigorously controlled systems can be made workable, while a policy designed to guarantee full employment regardless of the supply price of labor and regardless of the demand for labor at given real wages must prove unworkable. Trying to make such a policy workable for a short period by generating inflationary movements of unexpected steepness has led us into profound difficulties, and it is imperative that we rid ourselves of these. Whether a system of generalized subsistence guarantees can prove viable depends on the characteristics of the population and on how such a system is constructed and administered. Thus, we may be hopeful about the future but we have a much better chance of overcoming our difficulties if we remain aware of the uncertainties and thereby of the dangers against which we must guard.

10. The Future of Macroeconomics

It does seem ·clear that in some essential respects the macro-theoretical systems of the future will have to possess different properties from those in which our students have been trained. When we try to visualize future developments in the area of economic theory, it is advisable not to take into account the possibility that the United States (or any other major Western country) will for a long time be lost and demoralized in an area of haphazard and ineffectual interferences under partial government controls administered with a view to the next election. If that possibility should turn out to be the case, its intellectual counterpart is likely to be represented by bizarre and basically uninteresting variants of Keynesianism. The possibility cannot, of course, be entirely disregarded, but for our present purposes we may leave it aside.

A rigorously controlled economic and political system needs a demand management theory whose role is much less central in the general analytical structure than has been the role of our demand theories in recent decades. In such a system demand management becomes a handmaiden of comprehensive administrative planning, probably with subsidies as well as rigorous price controls included in the planning operations, and thus with inflation and deflation much less a problem. In these systems the difficulties to which the population is exposed develop mainly from a very high degree of dependence of the individual on those in charge politically. It is this power structure that, in the specific area of economic affairs, reflects itself in a low level of innovating activity and in a lack of adjustability of the product mix to the desires of the public.

If we are to prove successful in avoiding these developments, we must rely on a macro-theoretical framework that clearly recognizes the price level implications of the concept of macro-equilibrium. To do so will require recognition of the dependence of workable demand policy on a strategy by which price level expectations are conditioned to policy targets. In addition, the effect of widely spreading subsistence guarantees must be recognized much more clearly. In other respects, too, it will be necessary to pay more attention to the bearing of institutional rigidities on achievable employment policy goals. One may favor some of these rigidities—all of us probably favor some and take some others for granted even if we do not favor them—but in that case one must accept their consequences and leave room for them in one's macro-theory and employment policy. Other institutional rigidities exist largely because the bulk of the public misunderstands their consequences and has not been made properly aware of the harm they do.

If we are to succeed in avoiding unpalatable political and economic alternatives, we shall need a macro-theory assigning the proper role to the problems this volume addresses. Differently expressed: *unless* we develop our analysis in a framework recognizing the significance of these problems, we shall before long witness basic changes in our economic and political environment, and these changes will have become acceptable only because we shall by then have moved into an area of low performance and demoralization.

Numbered References

[1] Brunner, K., and Meltzer, A. H. "Friedman's Monetary Theory." In R. J. Gordon, ed., *Milton Friedman's Monetary Framework*. Chicago, Ill.-London: University of Chicago Press, 1974.

[2] Cagan, P. *The Hydra-Headed Monster*. Washington, D. C.: American Enterprise Institute, 1974.

[3] Council of Economic Advisers. *Annual Report*. Washington, D. C.: Government Printing Office, January 1975.

[4] ———. *Annual Report*. Washington, D. C.: Government Printing Office, January 1976.

[5] Davidson, P. "A Keynesian View of Friedman's Theoretical Framework for Monetary Analysis." In R. J. Gordon, ed., *Milton Friedman's Monetary Framework*.

[6] Eckstein, O., and Brinner, R. *The Inflation Process in the United States*. Washington, D. C.: Joint Economic Committee, 92nd Congress, 2nd session, 1972.

[7] Fellner, W. "Two Propositions in the Theory of Induced Innovations." *Economic Journal*, June 1961.

[8] ———. "Phillips-Type Approach or Acceleration?" *Brookings Papers on Economic Activity*, 1971(2).

[9] ———. "Empirical Support for Induced Innovations." *Quarterly Journal of Economics*, November 1971.

[10] Fisher, I. "A Statistical Relation between Unemployment and Price Changes." *International Labor Review*, June 1926.

[11] Friedman, M. *A Theory of the Consumption Function*. Princeton, N.J.: Princeton University Press, 1957.

[12] ———. "The Optimum Quantity of Money." Essay No. 1 in M. Friedman, *The Optimum Quantity of Money and Other Essays*. Chicago, Ill.: Aldine Publishing Co., 1969.

[13] ———. "The Role of Monetary Policy." Essay No. 5 in M. Friedman, *The Optimum Quantity of Money and Other Essays*. Reprinted from *American Economic Review*, March 1968.

[14] ———. "A Theoretical Framework for Monetary Analysis." In R. J. Gordon, ed., *Milton Friedman's Monetary Framework*.

[15] ———. "Comments on the Critics." In R. J. Gordon, ed., *Milton Friedman's Monetary Framework*.

[16] Friedman, M., and Schwartz, A. J. *A Monetary History of the United States*. A Study by the National Bureau of Economic Research, New York. Princeton, N.J.: Princeton University Press, 1963.

[17] Goldfeld, S. M. "The Demand for Money Revisited." *Brookings Papers on Economic Activity*, 1973(3).

[18] Gordon, R. J. "The Recent Acceleration of Inflation and Its Lessons for the Future." *Brookings Papers on Economic Activity*, 1970(1).

[19] Haberler, G. *Prosperity and Depression*. Cambridge, Mass.: Harvard University Press, 1937, 4th rev. ed., 1958.

[20] ———. *Economic Growth and Stability*. Los Angeles, Calif.: Nash, 1974.

[21] Hicks, Sir John. "Mr. Keynes and the Classics." Reprinted from *Econometrica*, 1937. In W. Fellner and B. F. Haley, eds., American Economic Association, *Readings in the Theory of Income Distribution*. Philadelphia-Toronto: Irving, 1946.

[22] ———. *A Contribution to the Theory of the Trade Cycle*. London: Oxford University Press, 1950.

[23] Hutchison, T. W. *Economics and Economic Policy in Britain 1946–1966*. London: Allen and Unwin, 1968.

[24] Kahn, R. F. (Lord Kahn). "The Relation of Home Investment to Unemployment." *Economic Journal*, June 1931.

[25] Kennedy, C. "Induced Bias in Innovation and the Theory of Distribution." *Economic Journal,* September 1964.

[26] ———. "Samuelson on Induced Innovations." *Review of Economics and Statistics,* November 1966.

[27] Keynes, J. M. (Lord Keynes). *The General Theory of Employment, Interest and Money.* London-New York: Macmillan, 1936.

[28] Leijonhufvud, A. *Keynesian Economics and the Economics of Keynes.* New York-London-Toronto: Oxford University Press, 1966, 2nd ed., 1968.

[29] Lucas, R. E., Jr., and Rapping, L. A. "Real Wages, Employment, and Inflation." *Journal of Political Economy,* September/October 1969.

[30] Marshall, A. *Money, Credit and Commerce.* London: Macmillan, 1923.

[31] Modigliani, F., and Brumberg, R. "Utility Analysis and the Consumption Function: An Interpretation of Cross-Section Data." In K. K. Kurihara, ed., *Post-Keynesian Economics.* New Brunswick, N. J.: Rutgers University Press, 1954.

[32] Mundell, R. A. "Capital Mobility and Stabilization Policy under Fixed and Flexible Exchange Rates." *Canadian Journal of Economics and Political Science,* November 1963.

[33] Okun, A. M. "A Review of Some Economic Forecasts for 1955–57." *Journal of Business,* July 1959.

[34] ———. "Inflation: Its Mechanics and Welfare Costs." *Brookings Papers on Economic Activity,* 1975(2).

[35] Patinkin, D. C. *Prices, Interest and Money.* Evanston, Ill.: Row-Peterson, 1956, 2nd ed., New York: Harper & Row, 1965.

[36] ———. "Friedman on the Quantity Theory and Keynesian Economics." In R. J. Gordon, ed., *Milton Friedman's Monetary Framework.*

[37] Perry, G. L. "Changing Labor Markets and Inflation." *Brookings Papers on Economic Activity,* 1970(3).

[38] Phelps, E. S. "Money Wage Dynamics and Labor Market Equilibrium." In E. S. Phelps et al., *Microeconomic Foun-*

dations of Employment and Inflation Theory. New York: W. W. Norton, 1970.

[39] Phillips, A. W. "The Relation between Unemployment and the Rate of Change of Money Wage Rates in the United Kingdom, 1861–1957." *Economica,* November 1958.

[40] Pigou, A. C. "The Classical Stationary State." *Economic Journal,* December 1943.

[41] Samuelson, P. A. "Interaction between the Multiplier Analysis and the Principle of Acceleration." *Review of Economics and Statistics,* May 1939. Reprinted in Joseph E. Stiglitz, ed., *P. A. Samuelson, Collected Scientific Papers,* vol. 2. Cambridge, Mass.: M.I.T. Press, 1966.

[42] _____. "A Theory of Induced Innovations along Kennedy-Weizsäcker Lines." *Review of Economics and Statistics,* November 1965. Reprinted in Robert C. Merton, ed., *P. A. Samuelson, Collected Scientific Papers,* vol. 3, 1972.

[43] _____. "Rejoinder: Agreements, Disagreements, Doubts, and the Case of Induced Harrod-Neutral Technical Change." *Review of Economics and Statistics,* November 1966. Reprinted in Robert C. Merton, ed., *P. A. Samuelson, Collected Scientific Papers,* vol. 3, 1972.

[44] Sargent, T. J. "Rational Expectations, the Real Rate of Interest, and the Natural Rate of Unemployment." *Brookings Papers on Economic Activity,* 1973(2). See also a correction in *Brookings Papers on Economic Activity,* 1973(3).

[45] Sargent, T. J., and Wallace, N. "Rational Expectations and the Theory of Economic Policy." *Studies in Monetary Economics 2.* Minneapolis, Minn.: Federal Reserve Bank of Minneapolis, June 1975.

[46] Sohmen, E. *Flexible Exchange Rates.* Chicago, Ill.: University of Chicago Press, 1961.

[47] Sweeney, R. J. *A Macro-Theory with Micro Foundations.* Cincinnati, Ohio: Southwestern Publishing Co., 1974.

[48] Tobin, J., "Liquidity Preference as Behavior Towards Risk." *Review of Economic Studies,* February 1958.

[49] _____. "Inflation and Unemployment." *American Economic Review,* March 1972.

[50] ———. "Friedman's Theoretical Framework." In R. J. Gordon, ed., *Milton Friedman's Monetary Framework*.

[51] Walras, L. *Elements of Pure Economics; or, The Theory of Social Wealth*. Translation and commentaries by William Jaffe. Homewood, Ill.: Richard D. Irwin, 1954.

Index

147

Cover and book design : Pat Taylor